GLORIOUS SURRENDER

FINDING THE TREASURE HIDDEN IN TRIALS

STACEY WEEKS

GLORIOUS
SURRENDER

Stacey Weeks

CHANGED BY GRACE · CHANGED BY LOVE

PRAISE FOR GLORIOUS SURRENDER

In Glorious Surrender, Stacey Weeks writes with transparency about the tension and the transformation that her role as a pastor's wife played in bringing her to the place of ultimate freedom—one who seeks God's glory above all else. She communicates with honesty about the messiness of real life in public ministry, and takes readers on a journey through raw life topics including pride, living authentically, finding true rest in the chaos, and spiritual warfare. Her passion for God's glory to preoccupy and transform everyday living accompanies every thought on every page. This book is not just for pastors' wives, it is for women wanting to take a vulnerable look at the sins and deceptions that lurk within their minds and hearts that can stall their progress toward finding true purpose. A must read!

— ANDREA THOM, AUTHOR OF RUTH: REDEEMING THE DARKNESS AND AMOS: COME AWAKE!

Often we sit in our seats and wonder what the life of our pastor is like but forget that there is another person in that relationship that must honour the God-given calling of that man. Glorious Surrender is more than Stacey's story; it is about God's ability to shape any ordinary person into the image of Him.

— KEVIN MILLER, CHURCH ELDER

If you want to glorify God in everything you think, say, and do, I recommend reading Glorious Surrender.

— TAMI SWARTZ, BIBLICAL COUNSELLOR

*For Kevin, who boldly followed the Lord
and led his family well even when it was difficult.
I love you.*

*So, whether you eat or drink, or whatever you do,
do all to the glory of God.*

1 Corinthians 10:31

FREE SHORT STORIES
FREE SHORT STUDIES

Snag free short stories and studies
by Stacey Weeks
StaceyWeeks.com/free-shorts/

CONTENTS

FOREWORD

In the midst of a culture where individualism and independence reign, the subject of true surrender will stand out as a light in the darkness. The flesh inside us fights ferociously against surrender, but the Spirit of God in us delights in it. Furthermore, what the genuine heart will discover is that true surrender before the Lord Almighty is where life and love are sincerely found. That is why Glorious Surrender is such a timely and needed book.

Consider the life-changing, world-altering words of surrender made by Jesus Christ: "Not my will, but yours be done" (Luke 22:42). In this one phrase, Jesus powerfully set aside His will to follow in perfect faith, obedience, and yes, surrender to His Father. The result of this divine submission was the giving of His life beyond what we can imagine.

That's why surrender is so precious and powerful. Surrender before the Lord ushers in God's grace, strength, and joy. It's counterintuitive, but surrender leads to a life of abundance.

So many will miss out on supernatural freedom because they are unwilling to release control of their lives to the One who holds it all. This is why Jesus also said, "Unless a grain of wheat falls into the earth and dies, it remains alone; but if it dies, it bears much fruit" (John 12:24). It was true for the life of Jesus Christ as He gave up His life on the cross, and it is true for all of us who are called to follow Him.

Glorious Surrender is a wonderfully written and passionate call to women. Stacey Weeks has unveiled her own heart and how the Lord has moulded her, broken her, and transformed her through surrender. She shares intimately her own experience and how it has brought her deep wells of joy. She deeply desires you to know and live in the same truth.

This book is specifically written with women in mind and therefore is full of insights and wisdom that women of all ages will find deeply relevant. No doubt you'll be nodding your head as you go through each chapter. Glorious Surrender will renew your mind and touch your heart.

I appreciate how Stacey has beautifully balanced grace and truth and seeks to practically apply the principles within. Read this book, be blessed, and encourage others to do the same. It is a privilege and a pleasure for me to recommend this book as a powerful tool of discipleship on the subject of critical importance in our day.

—Robbie Symons

Pastor and author of *Passion Cry*

HOW TO USE THIS STUDY

When the idea first stirred in me to explore womanhood fully surrendered to God, I resisted. I'm a fiction writer. A storyteller. I read and write to escape the hardships of reality, not immerse myself in the trenches of it. Furthermore, I didn't want to look deep inside myself and address the fears and difficulties that accompanied a complete surrender to the Lord. I wasn't sure if I could relinquish my heart completely and remain unscathed.

But it turned out that this storyteller had a story to tell about what I wish I knew as a young woman seeking to love God with my whole heart. It's about how God requires surrender from His children. It's about how He uses broken people, even if He has to break them Himself to make them useful.

God loved me too much to leave me to my self-centred ways. He crushed my prideful and idolatrous heart, exposed my greed, and allowed shattering trials to come my way. Then He took the pieces that remained and shaped me into something beautiful and useful to Him. He can do this for you, too.

Broken dreams can be the catalyst that sparks a search for deeper intimacy with the Lord. They are evidence of our need, prompting us to shamelessly call out to Him for grace, mercy, and restoration and lay it all at His feet in complete surrender.

How to Use this Book

There are thirteen chapters in Glorious Surrender. The first nine include my struggle with the chapter's topic and how the Lord led me to surrender. We will journey together through these nine chapters. They contain reflection questions designed to prompt deeper thinking and personal application. These can be done alone or in a group.

The remaining chapters begin with an encouragement and end with an exhortation. They include five passages of Scripture along with study questions designed to walk you through the text and apply everything you have learned about suffering, surrender, and God's sovereignty.

Time Requirements

Although you can read Glorious Surrender straight through as an encouraging message of hope during hardships, I recommend taking your time, completing one chapter a week. The study can be used individually, but if possible, invite some women to join you so you can learn and be encouraged together.

The Goal

As you yield to God, He will usher you into an emotionally charged, exhilarating, life-altering season of life. The very things you fear — confessing and admitting sin, exposing your inner heart, letting go of control, you-fill-in-the-blank — can become an incredible blessing as you relinquish yourself to the Lord and follow His leading. In the process of examining what it means to live fully surrendered to God as a woman, a wife, a mother, a sister, a daughter, and a friend, you'll see that God uses everything for good.

Everything, even those fractured years included in my story.

God is writing our lives to bring glory to Him. You may not be married to a pastor like I am, or even married at all. Maybe you've struggled with fertility like me, or maybe you have half a dozen kids under the age of six. Maybe you've suffered great, unimaginable loss. Your circumstances might be vastly different from mine, but we both have pages in God's story. God is writing your life to bring glory to Him. He is asking you to do the same thing He asks all His children to do: surrender. Completely surrender. So, whether we eat or drink, or whatever we do, we will do it all to the glory of God.

1

BROKEN BEAUTIFULLY

*T*he greatest danger to ministry is me. When Pastor Todd Dugard spoke those words, he mostly spoke to those serving as senior pastors. However, his words rolled around in my mind, sinking deep. Soul-achingly deep.

I am the greatest danger to the ministry to which God has called me. And similarly, you are the greatest danger to whatever purpose God has called you to fulfill.

When God led my pastor-husband in a new direction, leading our family into a season of change, I dug in my heels and resisted with gross negativity.

I will not uproot our kids and move, I insisted. I will not leave our home. I will not spend an entire year in constant transition.

I. Will. Not.

I refused to yield to the clear direction of God.

Instead of being a helpmate to my spouse, I became an obstacle in his obedience to the Lord. I am ashamed that I didn't embrace and affirm the calling of God in his life. I am overwhelmed by God's mercy and how He didn't allow me to block His work in my husband. I thank God for wrestling me to the ground and breaking my pride-filled, sinful heart.

I vividly remember the day I realized all the plans I had made for my life were about to change. I faced off with God. I roared about this unexpected upheaval and how it felt terribly unfair. I listed all the things I loved about our life that I didn't want to give up. And God, in an act of incredible grace toward me, dropped me at a crossroads where I had to choose between Him and me. I had to choose between bravery and fear, faith and doubt, obedience and selfishness.

God softened my heart and brought me to repentance. Repentance didn't erase my sorrow or fear about the unavoidable and imminent changes, and it didn't usher in excitement about the upcoming year. Still, it enabled me to yield all my desires and dreams to God so I could walk in obedience to Him. I left my God-encounter shattered, ready to be the wife He called me to be, ready to follow wherever He leads. God had broken my will and exposed the filthy sin inside my self-righteous heart.

It would be great if I could say that this was the only time I've struggled with obedience to God, but it isn't. I've wrestled down selfish tendencies multiple times. I've experienced the consequences of the achingly true and ugly words that my sin is the greatest danger to me and to the work God has called me to accomplish.

At times, I am painfully aware of my tendency to be selfish and proud, even when appearing to assist others. Whether it's serving the church or helping my family, too often, I wonder about my needs, how I feel, and how I look.

This selfish seed grew into a belief that I deserved more than the sacrifices life required, that I deserved more than the sacrifices motherhood required, that I deserved more than the sacrifices God required. But, in another act of great mercy toward me, God opened my eyes to the fallacy of those thoughts. When we are full to the brim of self, there is no room for God, making it far too easy to twist the things we intend to do for the Lord until they serve us.

God's Word reveals a consistent pattern of Him asking His followers to shift their eyes from themselves and fix them on Him. In the book of Joshua, we read how Rahab forfeited her safety and offered the remains of her used and broken life to conceal the Israelites spies. In Esther's book, we read how she trusted God to prepare her to step out in faith even though it could result in her death. Throughout the Gospels, we read of Mary's obedience. She embraced a life of ridicule and shame, all for God's purposes and our ultimate good.

These women quietly did as the Lord requested. They offered themselves to God and invited Him to do what He needed to accomplish His good and perfect plan. Perhaps, if we seek God's face during current trials, we will see that it's from those charred ashes, from the burnt offering of self, that God often creates something new and even more beautiful than before.

Rahab's life dramatically changed for good when she vowed to follow the one true God. God used Esther to save His people from destruction. Through Mary, God brought into the world the One who would deliver us from our sins. If God accomplished His will through their obedience and complete surrender, consider what He might accomplish through our obedience and surrender.

Even Christ learned obedience from what He suffered, so there is little hope that we will learn obedience differently. We fix our eyes on God and prepare our hearts to sacrifice, or we forfeit the blessing. How much more would Christ have been glorified through me if I had endured the pain of unjust suffering and entrusted myself to His care? I've come to suspect that the difficulties God allowed in my early married years had less to do with fairness and more to do with the sifting of my heart. God used hardships and what I perceived as injustices to expose my sin.

Oh, how we need more of Christ and less of us. We need to long for the day when the struggle within will cease, and we will spend eternity in pure worship of Him. But, until that beautiful day, the battle rages. The daily sacrifice of self will cycle on and on. Each morning we must decide if we are willing to set down our wants, desires, and needs and instead pick up what God has for us. Will we set down ourselves, what we perceive to be fair, and pick up our cross? Will we renounce everything to be His disciple (Luke 14:33)?

There is a cost to following Jesus (Luke 14:26-33). His gift of salvation is free, but we forfeit our rights and willfully submit to Him in accepting it. Following Christ might cost us relationships, ambitions, and possibly our lives. That is the truth. Trying to claim happiness, comfort, or health as part of God's promised plan on earth is a false, feel-good gospel destined to disappoint. In the complex and emotional moments of suffering, our hearts must submit to the truth revealed in the Word.

One way or another, we break. Perhaps under the strain and stress of trying to maintain impossible standards that over time hardens a heart until it falls and shatters. Maybe under the correction and discipline of a God who loves us too much to let us continue on a path of self-focused living. Maybe through reaping the natural consequences of sinful seeds sown in haste. Or maybe, under the tender pressure of God's hand, shaping us through the constant sanding of rough edges and bending of wills. We will break. But it is better to be broken by God for His purposes than shattered by the world and left in pieces. Being broken for Him is worth it.

Christ knows how it feels to be broken. His slashed flesh and spilled blood pierced the very heart of God. Jesus's obedience cost much. He asked God to find another way on the eve of His surrender, in the garden of Gethsemane. Still, He willingly went with His enemies. He experienced the wrath of God, so we don't have to. He took our sin upon Himself so that we can stand before God forgiven, and He wants us to live as He did. He willingly went into the hard places in obedience and submission to God. He wants us to love others with the same costly love that withholds nothing.

It is so much harder in practice. But God never promised easy; He promised Himself. Do I believe that He is enough when the stakes are high? Will I, like Rahab, trust God to use a sinner like me to accomplish His plan? Will I, like Esther, believe He has prepared me to step out in faith even if it costs me everything? Will I, like Mary, obey God even if it results in ridicule? Will you? Or is that just fancy church talk that tickles the ears but fails to penetrate the heart?

In so many ways, I am afraid suffering will overwhelm me. I don't want a risky life or risky love. I want safe ministries. Safe friends. Safe children. I want a secure future free of risk, hurt, and heartbreak. But Christ isn't safe. He is uncontainable, unstoppable, untamed, and all-powerful. He isn't safe, as author C.S.

Lewis says in The Lion, the Witch, and the Wardrobe, but He is good.[1] When He enters into our lives, our world turns upside down. This God of immeasurable greatness asks us to die to ourselves so that we might truly live. He asks us to forfeit earthly treasures to store up treasures in heaven. He asks us to daily surrender all the things we love, inviting Him to take and use whatever He pleases to accomplish His will. Is it safe? No. Is it good? Yes!

The real truth is that some of God's greatest blessings are hiding behind that thing that is difficult to surrender. We must move out of our safe circles and risk for Him. We must love even when it is hard. We must love like God and enter in, risking all of ourselves for His glory.

He didn't just love us from afar; He came into our world, and entered into our pain, and joined us on earth so He could love us through our journey. It is impossible to love from a distance. Love is an act of entering in. Love is an act of obedience that surrenders all of life to Him, even if it presents itself in pieces.

God wants the splintered remains from that difficult season when my husband and I almost gave up and left the ministry for good. He wants the pieces I've hidden away, the broken shards of failure that I haven't shared with anyone because the pain is too deep. He wants the pieces coloured in shame over words spoken aloud and the words uttered in the dark, fleshly folds of my conscience. He wants the pieces that feel impossible to surrender. He wants what shattered on the way down from the mountain top, when the struggle intensified, when the enemy attacked, and the road became impossibly narrow.

When we give Him those pieces, the ache to be faithful overcomes the ache to give up. He gathers us in His punctured hands. His grip tightens. He presses in, never letting go. Piece by devastated piece, He builds something new, something that never would've been without the broken wounds that burrowed even deeper into Him. He prepares something good for us. Each splinter epitomizes His love, His mercy, and His promise to restore.

By His strength, we can inch away from safe and move toward Him. We can learn to live dangerously, trusting like Rahab, loving like Esther, and obeying like Mary, totally dependent upon Him. As God's daughters, His Spirit lives within us, leading us through those hard places to bring Himself glory. He displays His goodness and divine character to the world through us. This brings Him pleasure, deepens our intimacy with Him, and reveals His glory. That is His plan, His will, His purpose in our trials.

We must pray that His character will manifest in us regardless of the outcome. We must fix our eyes on Him and allow no earthly comfort to come between us. We must fervently pray for God's will to be done in our minds, in our hearts, in our lives. When we are vulnerable for Him, expressing our need and trust in His limitless ability, expressing our settled belief that He is good regardless of the outcome, this broken and dying world sees Jesus. In the midst of that desperate and earnest prayer, the broken becomes beautiful, all for His glory.

PRAYER

O Lord, I long to represent You well. I want Your character to manifest in me regardless of my circumstances. So I will fix my eyes on You and reject earthly comforts that threaten to come between us. But I need Your help. Because Your Spirit is alive in me, I have everything within me that I need to obey Your commands. Remind me of this truth in my moments of desperation.

— FOR YOUR GLORY

REFLECTION QUESTIONS

1. What are you clutching in your hand that God is calling you to offer as a sacrifice to Him? What practical change can you make toward releasing it?

2. Examine your heart and ask the Lord to reveal to you why you are unwilling to surrender obediently: are you afraid, selfish, proud, anxious, or lacking in knowledge? Name two areas in which you find surrender difficult and identify the barrier to surrendering.

3. Develop a counterattack plan to combat me-centred thinking such as Scripture memory, prayer, meeting with an accountability partner, and worship. Write out the verses you need to memorize. Write down what attitudes and actions you need

to take off and what attitudes and actions you need to put on to facilitate this change (Ephesians 4:17–32).

4. Recount God's past faithfulness and praise Him for the work He has done through and around you. Make a list.

5. What could God be trying to sift in your heart through your current trials and suffering? Tell one person and ask them to pray for you.

6. Is Christ your true joy and your all-in-all, or are you placating yourself with someone or something else? What two steps can you take to correct this?

Your Thoughts

Your Thoughts

_____

_____

_____

_____

_____

_____

_____

_____

_____

_____

_____

_____

_____

_____

_____

_____

_____

_____

2

A MESSY LIFE

*M*ost days, I will be quick to say that I love my life serving God as a ministry wife. It's a messy, unpredictable, flawed, and intensely demanding life. I love where God has directed our family, and I love the way He grips the hearts of our children and shapes them into His image. I love the way He uses hardships to drag my eyes back to Him, where they belong. I love being brought to the exhausted end of myself, so when His great plans arrive, I undoubtedly know it was all His work and not mine. I am overwhelmed by the privilege of being used by God. I'm overwhelmed at the grace He lavishes upon me. It is a complete joy to live this life for Him.

But there are other days. Darker days. There are days when the attitude shifts inward, and I focus too much on the discomfort of this world rather than the glory to come. There are hard days when the reality of being married to my pastor and having few people who genuinely understand the heavy demands of ministry life threaten to overwhelm me. There are days when I want to unburden myself on my husband but know he cannot possibly shoulder another weight. There are days when I want to discuss the heavy issues pressing in but can't because they are confidential. There are days when I'm frustrated, but I don't want to tarnish my husband's, our church's, or my reputation by displaying my feelings. There were even days when I wanted to turn back, get off, bailout, and buckle under in my early ministry years because it all felt like a performance.

That dance of perfection demanded everything of me. It required all my time, all my energy, and all my resources. When I poured myself empty to maintain appearances, poured myself empty seeking approval from others, poured myself empty in an attempt to impress, it sapped my joy, leaving nothing. It left nothing for God and nothing for my family. Nothing.

But God is not calling us to perfection. Instead, He calls us to repentance. He calls us to humbly confess when pride crafts a picture of the ideal family, the ideal ministry, the ideal life or career, and when pursuing it with all our energy bumps God from the first place in our hearts. God, in His tender mercy, might allow our strain toward perfection to break us.

We might need to be broken to see our need to submit to His will and finally mean the words, "Not my will, Lord, but yours." We might need to be broken before we can choose to rejoice (Philippians 4:4-5). Choosing to rejoice was hard when the bills piled high, when parenting got tough, when my spouse was called out again, and I was left alone with the children. Choosing to rejoice was hard when unfair expectations weighed heavily on me, when my hopes were dashed, when I got everything I thought I wanted and still found it lacking. Choosing to rejoice was hard when God painfully sifted my heart and exposed the good things that had become god-things and now must become surrendered things.

Even this surrender wasn't accomplished in my strength. I needed to lay down the desire to surrender on my terms and fully surrender to God. He granted the desire to please Him as I sought Him. As I walked in obedience, relinquishing the longings of my heart, as I sought God through prayer and time in His Word, God showed me where to find that elusive joy He commanded me to have. Joy is the by-product of thankful prayers.

We need to fill our minds with His holy, living, and active Word. We must become vulnerable and invite trusted friends into our darkness to pray against the illusion of attainable perfection and confess the sins of jealousy, pride, and performance. God takes that picture we crafted and smashes it. He blows out the walls of our self-serving hearts, asking us to trust that He will collect the pieces as we confess, repent, and seek forgiveness. He restores us and makes us new. He fills us with peace and joy not based on circumstances or our ever-changing lives going our way but based on Him, our unchanging God who made Himself known through His Son, Jesus Christ. We will not find peace or joy in a perfectly groomed family, whether it's a church family, biological family, or adoptive family. They are found in Jesus and Him alone.

I am still in the cycle of confession, repentance, forgiveness, and restoration with God. I will be for the remainder of my earthly life because I am not a perfect woman. It can be very hard to be married to me. I am a sinful, broken woman saved by the grace of God. My husband is not a perfect man. It's sometimes hard to be married to him. As a sinful and broken man saved by the grace of God, he's on the same cycle as I am. If you think we have it all together just because we're in ministry, you need to take a closer look.

We are a mess. So don't be surprised when life with us, or anyone else, gets messy. But we love God with every piece of our broken, messy hearts and long to know Him and make Him known. I am continually overwhelmed by the awesome responsibility of serving a perfect God in an imperfect world. It cannot be done flawlessly, but the unfaultable God can take every humble offering and shape it and use it for His glory.

Life is hard. Family relationships are hard. Friendships are hard. They might hurt. They might even feel unfair. Living for Christ cost so much more than I expected. I had to surrender my plans for God's plans, believing His were best even if they were different. I had to surrender my dreams, desires, and hopes for the future and immerse myself in the lives of the people God placed around me, believing He had a purpose for our interaction that would glorify Him. Yet obedient surrender didn't promise ease.

When fallen, sinful people minister to fallen, sinful people in a fallen, sinful world, relationships get messy. Imperfect people clash. Sinful people hurt and get hurt. Ministry and family are places where emotions run high and opinions are strong.

However, they can also be beautiful places where these same imperfect people have an opportunity to connect with a perfect God, and through His grace, learn to love each other genuinely. They become places of joy when we serve one another through the power of a surrendered heart that values others above self. They are places where we acknowledge sin, recognize the discrepancies between who we are and who God calls us to be, and work toward change.

God knows that no one in my church, family, or social circles has it all figured out because He knows me. He knows the mess in my heart that wars between His will and mine. He knows my deeds, my thoughts, and the deepest longings of my soul. He knows them well. Before a word leaves my tongue, before a thought forms, before a step is complete, He knows, and He loves me anyway. He works in my heart, husband, family, and church, sifting and refining in uncomfortable ways that bring Him great glory.

He knows you, too. He knows your trials. He knows your loss. He knows your bone-achingly deep wounds that still bleed. He is working in your heart, sifting and refining you in uncomfortable ways that will bring Him great glory. I know because I've been there, smack in the middle of the mess, crying about the unfairness of it all.

And I've learned something very powerful: God doesn't function as we do. His ways and thoughts are higher than ours (Isaiah 55:9). God isn't bound by our limited, sinful understanding of fairness. God is greater, and He knows more than we ever will. He can do things that seem impossible and perhaps seem unfair and craft them into something beautiful. When we enter eternity, I doubt we will stand before Him and demand an explanation. I think that when we finally see God face-to-face, when we look upon Him in all His glory, we will fall at His feet in worship, fully knowing that He is worthy and we are not.

Pain reminds us that this earth is not meant to satisfy our deepest longings. This ache, this struggle, this difficulty, is temporary. It is, in part, designed to turn our eyes toward Him, recognizing our utter and complete dependence on His mercy. It is, in part, intended to whet our appetite for the glory to come. This messy earth is not our home.

Still, deep hurt is real. The raw emotion has humbled me, sent me scrambling for answers, and searching for God. It is from that viewpoint, from the low posture of humbly seeking God's face, that I have gained glimpses of God's plan. God has hidden slivers of peace and joy inside wounds that can only be found through submission and prayer. There is joy and opportunities to extend grace and offer forgiveness. There is joy in confession. There is joy in reconciliation.

There is peace in experiencing closeness with God, despite circumstances of overwhelming uncertainty. There is peace in surrendering our plans for His, our will to His. There is peace in asking God to reveal and carry for us the host of struggles we've been trying to lift on our own. All the correct theology in the world doesn't remove the pain of suffering—but it does bring peace. There is peace in knowing that God wastes nothing and will accomplish His purpose even in trials. Where we find His peace, we find His joy.

I am learning to search for those precious slivers hiding in pain. I'm learning more about the overwhelming ugliness of my sin and the constant battle between my sinful nature and the Holy Spirit. Then, when my pride convinces me I can handle things on my own, God peels back another layer of sin, and I see my smallness stand next to His greatness with fresh, humble eyes.

In many ways, I am just beginning to grasp how God has always been with me through trials. He is behind me, ahead of me, and with me right now. He is in my deep-aching despair. He is in my joyous celebration. Both gut-wrenching cries and songs of praise rise to Him as a fragrant offering of dependence. When our heart aches, His heart aches deeper. He loves His church, His bride, even more than our broken, desperate, invested hearts do.

I am thankful that God didn't give up on His creation when sin made a mess of the earth. I am grateful that He doesn't allow stubborn hearts to remain hard. I'm thankful that He is always good, even in the beautiful messes of ministry, life, and family.

Only God can take a mess like you and me and build something beautiful. Only God redeems regret, defeat, and history. As He refines our character through trials, we gain glimpses of the gracious, forgiving, and humble women He wants us to become. We gain glimpses of who He is shaping us to be and how we can't do it independently.

That's the beautiful part.

His strength and power transform our humble and willing hearts. Day-by-day, hour-by-hour, minute-by-minute, He will make us beautiful for His glory.

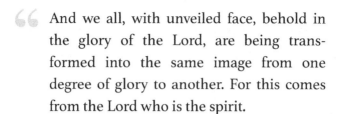

And we all, with unveiled face, behold in the glory of the Lord, are being transformed into the same image from one degree of glory to another. For this comes from the Lord who is the spirit.

— 2 CORINTHIANS 3:18

PRAYER

Lord, help me lay down my desire for
control, security, recognition, or what-
ever "it" is in my lives, not withholding
my broken hopes and dreams,
entrusting myself to the One who has
granted me far more than I deserve.
Prepare my heart to serve You with joy.
May I fall down and worship You while
You take the old away and create some-
thing new.

— FOR YOUR GLORY

REFLECTION QUESTIONS

1. Meditate on eternity with Christ. Spend 10 minutes in the Word, reading Revelation 21:1-7. Then, rewrite it in your own words.
2. Identify your dark-day triggers. Write down two thoughts that don't glorify God. Then, find and memorize a Scripture passage that refocuses your heart on Christ.
3. Spend some time in prayer, confessing, repenting and praising the Lord.
4. Look at your current mess. Where can you see God at work in your life, wanting to change and use you? Where can you see opportunities to glorify Him?
5. What has God revealed about Himself in this season (or a recent season) of difficulty? Name the wound or hurt that resulted from that season. For the next seven days, praise

God for working in you during that time.
Thank Him for walking with you through it.

6. List five joys you have been blessed with in
   current or past ministry opportunities.
   Thank God for them.

7. How does Isaiah 55:9 provide comfort when
   life is difficult? Write on a notecard two
   ways that Isaiah 55:9 provides comfort when
   life is difficult. Then, post the card in a
   visible place (like a refrigerator, mirror, on a
   window etc.).

Your Thoughts

_____
_____
_____
_____
_____
_____
_____
_____
_____
_____
_____
_____
_____
_____
_____
_____
_____
_____
_____
_____

Your Thoughts

_____

_____

_____

_____

_____

_____

_____

_____

_____

_____

_____

_____

_____

_____

_____

_____

_____

_____

_____

_____

_____

_____

3

IT'S NOT ABOUT ME

*L*ong before I took my first breath, God penned my story. Although I am in the narrative, my role is small. I am not the main character. I am not a hero. In some ways, I'm hardly a footnote at the bottom of the page. My story is more than a story about me; it's about something much bigger.

God the Father, God the Son, and God the Holy Spirit intimately designed a plan to weave our lives as a thread into their human story. We will never fully comprehend how or why the Triune God wrote us in. We have roles — roles that matter— yet it is not purely about us.

We often perceive that life, family, dreams, ministry, and talents are about us. How God must ache at such self-importance and pride. Everything that we are and all that we do is for God. He gives our lives purpose. Trials. Triumphs. Passion. Sorrows. Victories. Failures. Family. Dreams. Ministries. Talents. They all exist to bring Him glory. Our life's goal is to fulfil His purpose. I love the clarity my husband gave our church's core group right before our church plant launched into existence. He said,

> Jesus Christ is building His church. Not a man. Not a small group of people. Not a program. Only Jesus. There is great freedom in knowing that while we carry responsibility, it's ultimately not up to you or me.
>
> You may have been used in many God-glorifying, Christ-exalting, Holy Spirit-empowered ways, but remember, it's not up to you. It's up to Him. Only Jesus can build His church. Only Jesus will build His church.
>
> Rest in the truth that your loving, compassionate, sovereign Saviour knows what you need, when you need it, and how to best give it to you. Really, what better way is there to march into ministry? Anything of eternal value will happen only if He does it.
>
> Why? Because He has the name above every name, in this age but also in the one to come (Ephesians 1:21).

He is the head of the body, the church, the beginning, the firstborn from the dead, preeminent over all things (Colossians 1:18–19).

He is the radiance of the glory of God and the exact imprint of His nature, and He upholds the universe by the word of His power (Hebrews 1:3).

God lifts from us the responsibility to produce and places it upon the only shoulders capable of carrying it: His own. Understanding that we function by the power of Christ is wildly freeing, but still, I went years without fully grasping this truth.

When my husband and I first entered ministry together, I was unprepared for the expectations associated with the job of pastor's wife. Perhaps the unexpected expectations of wifehood, motherhood, ministry, or career have similarly blindsided you. Since I believed that building the church rested (to some degree) upon my shoulders, I allowed those expectations to shape my view of myself and direct my priorities. I believed our ministry success hinged on fulfilling my expected role, and I mentally twisted my responsibilities until everything revolved around me. What was I doing? Who was counting on me? What was expected of me? What was the pastor's wife supposed to do?

For many years, people's shifting opinions directed my life. I learned to play the piano, sing, lead Bible studies, be a speaker, lead crafts, be a prayer partner, meal bringer, best friend, counsellor, problem solver, Sunday school teacher, children's curriculum writer, and the list goes on and on. While there's nothing wrong with any of those activities, there was something very wrong with the heart attitude driving my actions. I was doing these things to please people, not out of love and service to God.

On some level, I knew it was wrong to allow others to wield so much power over my thoughts, emotions, and choices, but I craved acceptance and feared conflict. No matter how hard I tried to please everyone, I couldn't. It shattered me when a woman left our church because of a perceived failure of mine. It broke my heart when people expected me to address issues they had with my husband. It shocked me when I was criticized for singing too quietly for the people on the other side of the room to hear.

I was blind to the pride in my heart that caused me to believe that sheer determination and people-pleasing could produce spiritual results that pleased God. I had no idea what my role was, how to really study the Word, or how to pray against the ongoing spiritual battle for my affections. So I smiled more. I meddled in my husband's business. I sang louder. I had succumbed to the fear of man, and it had replaced my fear of God. When we fear man more than we fear God, we cease striving to please God and instead seek to please man. This is wrong.

Achieving success became an effort-based task dependent on my ability. If I worked hard enough, I should produce results. I removed God from my efforts and later wondered at my exhaustion and frustration. I ignored the most powerful weapons at my disposal — prayer and God's Word (Ephesians 6:11-20) — because I was too busy to do more than stop and offer a short and urgent prayer.

I went into battle unarmed and then cried over my wounds. My limited personal resources couldn't meet the significant needs of our community, let alone the great needs of the world. My strength was not strong enough. My wisdom was foolishness in God's eyes. I couldn't accomplish anything on my own, and when I tried, I crashed and burned. We left ministry uncertain if we would ever return.

In those months of recovery, of seeking God's face, of healing, repenting, and change, God reprimanded me. All things belong to Him because it is all about Him, not me. Only His ability can meet His desires and expectations. If I had worked as diligently on pleasing Him as I did on pleasing others, those early years could have been very different. True joy and peace are found only in a life fully surrendered to Jesus. They are not found in pleasing the unpleasable. They are not found in parenting perfectly groomed children. They are not even found in a life free of trials. Joy and peace are found in a life surrendered to Jesus because that's the only place where our trials have purpose. That is the only place where the tragic can be transformed and used for God's glory. That is the only place where lost years are redeemed, and new beginnings are created.

Our responsibilities in life are actually quite simple. We speak the truth with boldness. We lift high the name of Jesus. With thanksgiving and prayer, we make our requests known to God. We make disciples. It all boils down to a simple statement. We are to ensure that nothing comes between Jesus and us. Not the expectations of others. Not the expectations of self. Not a ministry we make about us. Our responsibility is walking in obedience to God and trusting the results to Him. Only God can produce God-sized results because God's unlimited resources never run dry. His strength never weakens. His wisdom founded the earth. His understanding established the heavens. By His knowledge, the deep broke open, and the clouds dropped down the dew (Proverbs 3:19–20). A successful life is defined by submission to Him.

To walk in this obedience, we need to learn to study, trust, and pray the Word of God at a depth that requires an investment of time, emotion, and passion. When we pray Scripture and cling to His promises in the difficult valley, trusting that He will build His church, God shifts our eyes from the brokenness of the earth to the glory to come. He isn't satisfied with child-like faith dependent on spiritual milk. He wants us to chew and digest the harder portions of His Word. He wants us to feed on the Word. He wants us to come to the end of ourselves so that He can become everything.

God will shape our character in those challenging stretches of moment-by-moment surrender, study, and perseverance. He will shape us when no one is looking but Him. He will press and fold and refine us where the battle rages beneath the surface, between each heartbeat.

There are questions every woman must face. Will I set aside what I want, crave, and plan to yield to God? What if it is hard? Terribly hard? Will I recognize and repent of the pride-filled heart lurking behind my desire for results and recognition? I suspect God is more interested in how we respond to the impositions that arise as we serve Him than He is in our impressive list of accomplishments. He is more interested in allowing trials to shape our character than in removing trials from our path. He loves us and desires personal intimacy with us, and He will use everything, even difficulty, to draw us closer to Him.

Every moment and thought must be taken captive, surrendered, and made obedient to Christ. Everything, including the hard things that no one else can see and the easy things that we'd like to believe don't matter. God is provider and sustainer. His grace is sufficient. We must set aside worries, obsessions, and plans and instead choose to praise His name for bringing us to a place of dependence on Him. Faith truly comes alive when we lay down anxiety and pick up His Word.

Humble prayers cried in intimate moments with God change us, and His everlasting love comforts us, not merely rebuilding us from brokenness, but re-creating us. Nothing is wasted. He knows our sorrow, pain, and need. He has collected our tears in a bottle. We cannot heal and restore our brokenness, but God can.

He does this not because there's anything worthy of redeeming in us but because He is a God full of grace who views us as righteous because Christ has imputed His righteousness on us. So it's not about us and what we have to give; it's all about Him and what He has done on our behalf.

I've never been able to find the security and peace I desire when I make everything about myself or how it affects me. Security and peace that truly satisfy are not found in obtaining, mastering, or conquering my dreams and desires. The answer is not in more of me, but less. I become less. God becomes greater. I must loosen my grip on those things that don't matter, things destined to burn until my love abides in Him and His in me, and I hold nothing back, loving uncon- ditionally, giving unreservedly, and forgiving entirely. When I give out of His strength until there is nothing left, He replenishes me. If I continually seek His replenishment, I will never run out because He never ever runs out.

In Him is the treasure I seek. I draw close to my Lord and hear His commands of love. I hear His promise to give me what I need to accomplish His commands.

My husband and I are still in full-time ministry, and I serve in a role I never thought I'd ever fill again. I'm risking my heart, emotions, and life to pour out genuine love for God's people. But this time around, the exhaustion is different. This time I know that the end of me is just the beginning of God. This time, as I yield to His direction, listen for His prompting, and pray without ceasing, He works through me. He feeds the hungry. He quenches their thirst. He clothes the naked. He comforts sick. He does much of it through me as I follow Him wherever and whenever He leads. I am doing it for Him because my life is centred on Him and completed in His strength.

Our God will never leave or forsake us because His character is consistent and does not change. We can trust our tomorrows to Him because He has proven faithful with our yesterdays. We can follow Him anywhere because this is His story, not ours. We can follow Him anywhere because He goes before us. He is not only building His church, but He is also building us, yet it is not about us. He does it all for His glory.

PRAYER

Lord, I believe that You will never leave me nor forsake me because Your character is consistent and does not change. I can trust my tomorrows to You because you've proven faithful with my yesterdays. I can follow You anywhere because this is Your story, not mine. I can follow You anywhere because You go before me. You're not only building your church, but I believe You are building me, and I know this is not about me. It is about You.

— FOR YOUR GLORY

REFLECTION QUESTIONS

1. List two areas in which you are enslaved to self-producing results. Ask your spouse, mentor, or trusted friend if they can help you identify areas of self-focus in your life.

2. Are you regularly in the Word and praying? Intimately knowing your Saviour is the best way to get the focus off yourself and onto His incredible grace and mercy, the lifeblood of a Christ honouring life. Set a goal regarding your time in the Word and ask someone to hold you accountable for one month.

3. Accolades from others are fleeting shadows. To what attitude change, schedule shift, or humble sacrifice is the Lord calling you in your current role to please Him first and foremost?

4. What do Colossians 1:18–20, and Hebrews 1:3 communicate about Jesus? Why does that matter?

5. In 1 Thessalonians 5:23-24, who controls the results of our service and obedience to God?

6. What does Proverbs 3:19–20 tell us about God's ability to accomplish His plans?

7. Look up two promises of God to encourage your heart when you fail or when others fail you. Post them next to your observations on Isaiah 55:9 from chapter 2, question seven.

Your Thoughts

_____
_____
_____
_____
_____
_____
_____
_____
_____
_____
_____
_____
_____
_____
_____
_____
_____
_____
_____
_____
_____
_____

Your Thoughts

4

LEAVE IT WITH GOD

*O*ur soul waits for the God of hope—our solid rock, our salvation, our fortress, our safe place—to do what He says He will do. He will be everything that we need. He will provide. He will deliver justice in His time. He is our Defender, Redeemer, and Friend. We will wait in full confidence because His foundation is firm and His resources never run dry. Our precious and most holy God knows the beginning and the end. Words cannot capture His majesty. He answers every prayer as He sees fit, so we pour out our hearts to Him over and over and over — as many times as it takes to leave our petitions in His hands. He never tires of our prayers. His strength never weakens.

But our strength does.

When the wait is long, the theology of trusting God is challenged by the difficulty of living it. In this exhausted spot, emotions must submit to sound doctrine, and that happens when the mind and heart are fully convinced that God is good, even when life is not. Loving and serving God cannot be contingent on getting our way, nor can it be swayed by changing feelings. We must resist the urge to snatch back our prayers through worry and anxiety and trust God regardless of the duration of our suffering. We must cling to what we know to be true: God is good. He loves us. He is sovereign. We must cling to the truth even when life is not good and circumstances tempt us to doubt.

Yet how many times have I taken back what I intended to leave with God? How many times have I tried to box Him into responses I preferred? How many times have I believed the lie that my right actions will prompt God to grant my desired results as if I could manipulate Him? Faith that is based on a God who delivers is easily shaken.

What happens if the slaves remain captive? If the sick die? If the lost are not found? What do I do with such questions? What do I do with my heated emotions when the captive, sick, and lost are my loved ones? Why does God say no? Are His answers fair? Is the purpose of life about fairness? How do unanswered questions and promises yet to be fulfilled fit together with 2 Peter 3:9?

 The Lord is not slow to fulfil his promise as some count slowness, but is patient toward

you, not wishing that any should perish,
but that all should reach repentance.

Difficult questions expose the more significant struggle of total surrender.

I have wrestled with complicated theology and how it affects my loved ones. If God chooses us, why doesn't He choose everyone? What responsibility lies with the individual? What does that mean for my unsaved loved one? If God is sovereign, why does He let our broken world shatter hearts and lives? Why doesn't He step in and change things? Why doesn't He come back now?

My finite mind cannot comprehend the infinite God, and so my inability to neatly fit everything together actually helps me remember His majesty and my proper place before him. I am the created; He is the Creator. He does not answer to me; I answer to Him. Therefore, I must work through difficult theology, trusting that "all Scripture is breathed out by God and profitable for teaching, for reproof, for correction, and for training in righteousness, that the man of God may be complete, equipped for every good work. (2 Timothy 3:16-17).

All Scripture, even the difficult passages that are harder to understand.

God wants us to know Him, which means learning more about Him so that our hearts can respond in alignment with His Word — regardless of our circumstances. The deeper we know the Lord, the greater we grow in our love for Him. For our hearts to genuinely love God and feel safe in His hands, we must know Him.

The only way to know Him intimately is by studying the Word and working through some of those difficult questions. Then, if we still don't understand, we can choose to trust God anyway because we know Him, and He is good. These are unchanging truths to which we must cling.

I could trust Him when we struggled through years of infertility. I could trust Him when ministry experiences soured our hearts. I could trust Him as we stood by the hospital bed pleading for mercy. I could trust Him when the diagnosis was grim. I could trust Him when He called my loved ones home long before I was ready to say goodbye. I could trust Him when it all felt horribly unfair. Why? Because only God is God.

He laid the earth's foundations, determined its measurements, stretched the line upon it, and laid the cornerstone with its morning stars that sang together. He shut in the sea when it burst from the womb. He prescribed limits to the proud waves and made them stay. He continues to command the morning and causes the dawn to know its place so that it might take hold of the skirts of the earth (Job 38). This is our God.

Even after years and years of praying, crying, and waiting expectantly on God, even after years of unchanged sameness, unchanged relationships, and unchanged health, I can choose to trust Him. I can trust Him because He is God, and He is good, even when life is terrible.

Some days it is hard to believe that God can make anything good rise from the ashes of a difficult season. When doubt beats down stronger than the prairie sunshine and evaporates the last dewdrop of faith, we must turn to Scripture. We must feed our minds with unchanging truths and the accounts of real people desiring to live in a way that honours their great God.

Scripture is full of people like you and me, regular people whose desire to please God compels and requires great faith that brings glory to God. Ordinary people are included in Scripture to comfort, challenge, and direct us to Christ.

When Shadrach, Meshach, and Abednego refused to give in to the temptation to save their lives by bowing down to King Nebuchadnezzar's golden statue, they were condemned to execution by a fiery furnace.

Flames have never threatened me, but I have been in fiery situations where I knew that God could redeem my situation, but I was also acutely aware that He might not. These men were right there, in that hard place where faith required action, and they responded without hesitation.

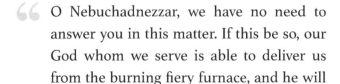 O Nebuchadnezzar, we have no need to answer you in this matter. If this be so, our God whom we serve is able to deliver us from the burning fiery furnace, and he will

> deliver us out of your hand, O king. But if not, be it known to you, O king, that we will not serve your gods or worship the golden image that you set up.

> — DANIEL 3:16-20

These words cut straight to my heart. Could God save them? You bet He could, but He might not. They had no idea how their trial would end, but they left their lives in God's hands anyway. Shadrach, Meshach, and Abed-nego declared before entering the furnace that even if God did not spare their physical lives, they would choose to obey Him. They understood that God was acting, even if He did not answer the way they expected or preferred.

Oh, how I need to learn this lesson! God's ways are so much higher than mine. His plan for me is so much bigger than I can understand. God doesn't need me nudging him along my timeline. My job is to surrender, obey, and follow Him one step at a time, regardless of how long I wait for the answer or whether the answer is what I want.

And when anguish finds its way into my small corner of life, it wrings the breath from my lungs. Trembling limbs fail, and howls of "why" rise from the pit. Why does God allow heartache? If He can, why does He sometimes not? I weep the great, weighty despair of sorrow because I do not know.

But I'll tell you what I do know. Our merciful God has caused us to be born again to a living hope through the resurrection of Jesus Christ from the dead. He's called us to an inheritance that is imperishable, undefiled, and unfading, kept in heaven for us and guarded by God's power, sustaining our faith. In this truth, we can rejoice despite being grieved by various trials. These trials test the genuineness of our faith, resulting in praise, glory, and honour to Jesus Christ (1 Peter 1:3–7).

My anguish tests the genuineness of my faith and accomplishes my deepest desire, bringing praise and glory and honour to Jesus Christ. So even when I don't understand what God is doing, God is good.

Still.

Always.

Never changing.

Good.

Even in the pit, He hears your cry. He can draw you out of the miry bog and set your feet up on the solid ground (Psalm 40:2).

There have been times in my life when I felt that my pain would bury me alive. Deep loss. Overwhelming fear. Unbelievable uncertainty. Scathing words. It all challenged my character and my love for the Lord, piercing my heart — but it was my wretchedness that broke it. My instinctive response to protect myself and pull back to lick my wounds and withhold submission, forgiveness, and mercy revealed the wretched woman I am (Romans 7:24).

I am not perfect, and neither are you. Because of that truth, at some point, life will hurt. At some point, the depth of your sin, your brother's sin, your sister's sin, or the general brokenness of the earth will devastate your heart, and it will hurt. Loss, shame, anger — it hurts. But if we establish God's trustworthiness and goodness in our minds and hearts before the fire rages, the flames will not consume us. They will hurt—but they won't destroy us. Decide now that because God is worthy and good and sovereign, you will obey regardless of the cost. Remind yourself now that His answer is better than yours. Decide now to live for His glory.

I prayed for relief from harsh and cruel treatment, but prayer didn't change the actions of those hurting me; it changed me. Although the enemy meant for those hard years to destroy me, God intervened within my fiery furnace. I learned that God's perfect plans and purposes were fulfilled *during* the confusion and scorching emotional pain. He had a different answer than I wanted to hear, one that was found by enduring the fiery furnace, not avoiding it.

After exiting those fiery trials, I learned something that I may have never fully grasped if I had been left untested. God's path might be the harder, narrower one to travel along, but the end goal of my life is not happiness or comfort. The end goal of my life is to glorify Him with my life. Sometimes what brings Him the most glory is how I conduct myself during trials, how I lean into Him and submit to His plan.

We don't endure lifes trials by doing our best. We endure by surrendering to God's will in trusting Him for His best. We won't emerge unscathed if we depend on our wisdom and resilience because it is not about surviving unscathed. But we can rest knowing that God is wise and dependable. Life is not about pushing through difficulty on human strength but about trusting God to provide one step at a time, one moment at a time, one breath at a time, even when we can't see where the path is heading. Trials may be more than you can handle, but they will never be more than He can handle.

You must believe.

I must believe.

We must believe.

The God who loves us, saves us, and hears our prayers acts on our behalf for His ultimate glory. God is the giver—providing everything we need. He is the forgiver, absolving the horrendous sins of our hearts, hands, and minds through the innocent blood of His Son. He is our help and our shield. Our hearts are glad in Him because we trust His holy name. We are safe in the palm of His hands. So let your heart take courage as you wait for Him.

PRAYER

*God, pour out Your grace upon me. Enable
me to wait on You in the suffering. Let
Your steadfast love be upon me as I hope
in You. Renew my mind so that my
heart can love You deeper. Renew my
strength so that I mount up with wings
as eagles, run and not grow weary,
walk and not faint.*

— FOR YOUR GLORY

REFLECTION QUESTIONS

1. What anxiety or cares are you tempted to snatch back from God's all-powerful sustaining hand? Why? What character trait of God, Scripture passage or biblical account can encourage you and bolster your faith to leave it with Him?

2. Write out a prayer of worship and praise, recounting the truth of who God is and of His great love and care for His own.

3. Pray now, asking the Lord to grow your faith so when the days of trial and temptation arise, you are armed with an intimate knowledge of the One who saves you forever for the glory of His name.

4. A popular misconception claims God will never give you more than you can handle. This is false. God often allows more than we

can handle, but it is never more than He can handle. With this in mind, what does it look like to turn from your strength and depend on God? Write down something that feels overwhelming to you and find Scripture that proves it is not more than God can handle.

5. Read 1 Peter 1:3–7. Do various trials grieve you right now? According to this passage, what does the trial accomplish in you?

6. Read Romans 7:15-25. How do you see this struggle manifest in your life?

7. Identify someone with whom you can pray and who will wisely and lovingly remind you of the goodness of God when the days are dark. Arrange to meet with the person for prayer.

Your Thoughts

_____

_____

_____

_____

_____

_____

_____

_____

_____

_____

_____

_____

_____

_____

_____

_____

_____

_____

_____

_____

_____

_____

Your Thoughts

_____

_____

_____

_____

_____

_____

_____

_____

_____

_____

_____

_____

_____

_____

_____

_____

_____

_____

_____

_____

5

THE FIGHT FOR TRANSPARENCY

*T*ransparency. The word alone makes my stomach roll. Over three decades into official adulthood, and I still feel the temptation to hide behind a veil. Every move and new friendship formed brought forth the same question: is this a safe place, or will they betray me? Terrifying uncertainties rip hope from my heart. Fearing disappointment, I slip behind the lonely veil of politeness that whisks me miles away from risky relationships.

This was my pattern for years. Hiding. Yearning for friendship, longing to be known but frightened of falling prey to disingenuous offers. My experiences as a ministry wife uncovered friends with secret agendas, friends who desired popularity with those in charge, friends who wanted a louder voice in church politics or a direct line to the pastor's ear. Despite many acquaintances who circled in and out of my life, I allowed few women into the deep folds of my heart, and I refused to journey with others into theirs. I then wondered at my isolation and unbearable loneliness that hollowed my heart with each beat.

The harsh truth that genuine friendships are rare became the glue upholding the barriers I labelled as boundaries. Every hurt became a brick on the wall enclosing my heart. These walls limited hurt but also held away love. My inability to forgive past wounds provided the enemy with a foothold and fostered foolish self-talk. No one was trustworthy. No one really cared. No one could handle the real mess of my life. Decade-old scars of betrayal were given reign, spewing salty lies that my ability to forgive offenders hinged on them seeking forgiveness and expressing genuine repentance. Bitterness rose within me, and I would wonder why I continued to sit in a pit of resentment and loneliness.

When you sink neck-deep into a preoccupation with self, the enemy celebrates. He knows how a focus on self stifles God's ministry through you. The enemy wants you to cower behind your wall of hurt and wallow in self-pity. He wants you to believe that you have protected the open wounds of loneliness, hurt, and rejection by staying there. Yet isolation and self-pity are never safe places. And if I linger in those lonely places and refuse to live a transparent life, why am I surprised or disappointed when others hide there as well? There is a deep longing for raw, real women in our communities. It is time to break down the walls and foster trustworthy spiritual intimacy.

How do you reveal the underbelly of your heart and protect it at the same time? Can you? Our communities are full of women, some desperately longing for authentic, mature, and genuine friendship. Someone must make the first move. Yet transparency is far more than answering the door makeup-free in your jammies. It also involves admitting the horrible fears we carry:

- Causing your repairable damage to our kids.
- Having that shameful event unearthed.
- Revealing that pain that brings you to tears every time it is mentioned.
- Confessing an unwillingness to forgive past hurts.

It's more than acknowledging that we need help because knowledge of our needs doesn't fix our needs. Instead, we must admit our wretchedness and turn to Jesus, asking Him to do what only He can do — change our hearts.

Authentic community is not admitting my failures and weakness and demanding that others accept me the way I am. Instead, it is looking at who I am, comparing it to who God desires me to be, acknowledging the discrepancies, and asking Him to change me. It involves asking for specific prayer and account-ability in those problematic areas. Authentic commu-nity invites someone else to speak hard truth into my struggles and preparing myself to be teachable to its instruction with grace.

We need friends who will challenge us to move outside of the comfortable, seek a closer walk with the Lord we adore, pray, minister, and love with fully invested hearts. We need friends who expect us to bring life's struggles before the throne and prayerfully intercede on their behalf regarding their struggles. The enemy wants us to miss this kind of accountability that spreads deep roots searching for living water. This kind of friend cannot be found in the safety of alone-ness. This kind of friend lives and breathes in commu-nity. It is hypocritical to crave and expect this from others while failing to exemplify it ourselves.

Someone must make the first move. Why can't it be me? Why shouldn't it be you?

Only by God's strength did I dip my trembling toe into the open space outside of my brick walls. By His strength, I agreed that sacrificing friendship and community was too high a price to keep paying. Although authentic friends and safe places were hard to find, I asked God to give me one true friend and help me be a true friend to someone else. And God worked His miracle of friendship on the other side of my boundary lines.

He opened my eyes to the women He had placed in

my life right now, who also seek Him, seek truth, and hide behind the same polite smile. These are the women who need what I need, authentic relationships that challenge one another to grow closer with the Lord. They are friends who will pray, minister, and love well. I pledged to the Lord that I would be the friend I longed to have. I want to see them grow in Christ, even if the necessary words to encourage that growth are hard to speak and even harder to hear.

This great leap of faith has not been easy, but it has been very good. I have come to openly love the women who walk with me through this process of sanctification. They don't expect perfection, often overflow with grace, and protect my confidences. I try to demonstrate the same to them. They know that I haven't become the person I thought I would become, and they accept me without judgement because the same is true for them. While we acknowledge the reality of right now, we crave more for ourselves and more for each other. We cheer each other onward as we leap into the terrifying unknown of authenticity, lifting our veils to speak the hard, honest truth. We are real friends who have scrubbed off the makeup and exposed the vulnerability caked in the wrinkles underneath. We are doing life together and know that it can't be done perfectly.

When others in our community fail us in their brokenness, we must seek rest in the One who will never fail to love and understand us exactly as we require. We are all imperfect. We are flawed and sinful.

We are caught in the middle of a war between our flesh and God's spirit. We won't always understand it right, respond right, or be right. At some point, we will likely fail our friends, just as they will probably disappoint us. We are all a collection of broken pieces in a broken world, and we want to be loved and put back together again with grace, mercy, and tenderness. It's when we fall to our knees and admit our lack, failures, weaknesses, and our longing for grace that we find hope in Jesus. Only He can meet every need.

Jesus takes our broken shards and shapes them into something new, declaring us His masterpiece. He chooses to journey with us and whispers to us that we are His beloved. He proclaims we are new, free, and forgiving. He calls us a friend, adopts us as daughters and makes us a co-heir with Him of His eternal kingdom. This union with Christ secures our inheritance because Jesus will not lose it.

We are the apple of His eye, His treasured possession, fearfully and wonderfully made. We are blessed. We are His. We are precious. Adored. Prized. Beloved. We can't earn it. We are not worthy of it. So we fall into the precious truths of our new identity and allow ourselves to *be loved*. Beloved. Love that is not based on who we are, but is based on who God is and will always be. It changes everything. The opinions of others matter less when we give God's opinion the full weight He deserves.

He is the friend who sticks closer than a brother

and carries us when others fail. His opinion is the only one that matters. When we know who God is and the value He has ascribed to us based on Jesus' payment for our sin, we can bravely pour into the women God places in our lives. We can invest right now rather than wait for more "adequate" relationships that may never arrive. We can be trustworthy friends to someone right now. We can carefully handle the hearts that are broken open to us. We can lead others toward life and rest in God's strength to accomplish His purposes. We can ask for His wisdom to find a friend and become a friend who acts in love.

So ask.

Ask your Lord for the community He has crafted you to thrive within. Ask Him for wisdom in finding a friend whose heart beats with His and shares your desire to make Him central. Ask to know Him better, love Him more, completely trust Him, and prioritize Him above all else. Ask Him for the community that will shape your shards into God-centred ends by speaking the truth in love. While you wait, rest in your Refuge and depend on His strength. Enjoy the One who is closer than a brother.

PRAYER

Precious Lord, give me eyes that see beyond
now. Give me feet that walk the hard
road of obedience while I wait for Your
provision. Give me a heart that beats in
time with Yours. When I feel like I am
climbing up a mountain and cannot see
You, give me faith to believe that You
are preparing to meet me at the peak.
When life doesn't unfold the way I
planned, help me remember that life is
not about me but about pouring into
others. I want to be the kind of friend
that I long to have. May it all be done
on Your strength.

— FOR YOUR GLORY

REFLECTION QUESTIONS

1. To whom is the Lord calling you to extend a heart of friendship? What does that look like practically? Write down two acts of service you can do to bless a new friend.

2. Commit to being an encourager to the sisters of the faith who God has placed in your life. First, write down three names of women you know or would like to know. Then, commit to praying for them. Now consider how you can encourage them with biblical truth. How will you connect with them? What specific questions can you ask them to get to know them better? How will you point them to the One who knits His church together for strength and purpose?

3. Are there any people to whom you are looking to meet needs that the Lord can

only fill? Repent of the sin of expecting a person to fill a role only God can fill.

4. Write down your unmet needs and ask God to show you through His word how you can depend on Him to meet these needs.

Your Thoughts

_____

_____

_____

_____

_____

_____

_____

_____

_____

_____

_____

_____

_____

_____

_____

_____

_____

_____

_____

_____

_____

_____

_____

_____

Your Thoughts

6

CONTENTMENT IS NOT HAPPINESS

$\mathcal{M}$y husband and I tried to have children for seven years before that prayer became a reality. Our lives were busy and quite happy, but we longed to be parents. Then, one day, we were invited to write a letter introducing ourselves to a young mother searching for a Christian family to adopt her child. She later narrowed her choice to us and one other couple.

I joyfully awaited her decision, certain she was an answer to years of prayer, certain this was God's blessing for us. There are no words to describe my devastation when she chose the other couple. I felt like God had let me down. Why had He let us go through this only to result in disappointment? I reminded God that we were faithful servants who had given up so much for Him. If God could do anything, why didn't

He grant us this child? I said things and asked questions that a lot of people voice when tragedy strikes.

But God was faithful, even when I was losing faith. He is good. His shoulders can handle my fears, feelings, and shattered dreams. He didn't crumble under my hard questions or retreat from my accusations. He didn't demand I censor my feelings. He invited me to bring it all to him, even the ugliness in my heart.

On that day, I had a choice. I could grow bitter because God had seemingly failed to deliver a right that I had claimed, or I could wrestle down the biblical command for contentment and learn what it means in devastating circumstances. Much like Abraham, I had to lay on the altar the thing I loved the most — my desire that had crept into the place reserved for God and God alone.

I learned that contentment isn't about getting my way. It's about my heart being right with God and rejoicing in the radical work He does for His glory.

My life belongs to God. All gifts come from Him, and I am His daughter. Everything I own and everyone I love belongs to Him to deal with as He sees fit. It must be surrendered.

Our whole lives, which include ministry, family, dreams and desires for the future, are for the glory of God. If we serve Him for any other reason, disappointment will destroy us. Until His glory is our purpose, until His will is our desire, until all we want is what He wants, it will cost too much. It will be too hard. It will cut too deep.

I remained terribly unhappy in our childless state. Yet, I could rejoice and trust that He would use my hurt for His purposes. I learned contentment and obedience through this suffering. I couldn't control our infertility. I couldn't control the outcome of that adoption, but I could control my response to the disappointment.

After wrestling with God and finally yielding my deepest longings to Him, I declared that He would be enough even if He never blessed us with children. A wave of happiness didn't surge through me at the declaration, but a tsunami of calm did. If a family was not part of His plan for our future, I could praise Him. I could speak of His goodness, faithfulness and love. I could take every opportunity to share how much He cares about the things I hold dear in my heart because He is enough. My love and trust in Him would not depend on how He answered my deepest desires. A sweet peace I had never known descended.

Years after submitting this desire to the Lord, He made way for us to adopt three beautiful children. But looking back, I am grateful that I submitted my heart to Him before He granted this dream. God chose, once again, to give me something I didn't deserve simply because He loved me. I didn't earn it. He didn't owe it to me. It was all grace.

What response do you need to control? With what

do you need to trust God? What if He says no? What if He says the gifts He gave you are not in preparation for some exciting future project but are for your current stretch of life, right now? Can my pride accept that God's perfect plan might limit the size of our church family for His purposes and our good? Can we accept that we are talented and gifted enough to succeed in big ways, but His plan might be about our success in small details? Can we accept His unknown sovereignty? Can we stop longing for a future plan to be fulfilled and joyfully serve God with all of ourselves right now? Can we honestly say it is all about Him and not about us?

The purpose of life is much grander than happiness. When we focus on glorifying God in plenty and need, we acknowledge that stuff doesn't bring contentment. Achieving long-held ambitions will not guarantee contentment. Earthly pleasures are intended to shift our eyes, gratitude, and praise to God for being the provider of all things. Our all-powerful God will never leave us or forsake us, and His presence with us all we really need. But it can be hard to win the battle between wants and needs. Before I arrived at that settled surrender, jealousy grew. When I noticed the blessings God gave others, both through offspring and material goods, resentment flourished. That covetousness grew larger and larger until God used Matthew 20:1–16 to remind my heart that He is a generous God. His gifts are not always equal, but they are always exactly what I need in my crisis moment to give Him glory.

I promised to live for God based on my great love for Him. The blessings He gave me are more than He ever promised. If He wanted to bless others with children, homes, and professional success, what business was it of mine? He could do what He wanted because He is God. Was I jealous because He loved others as much as He loved me?

Yes, I think I was.

When God provided me with a job, house, and ministry, I was happy and thankful. I was like the workers chosen by the vineyard owner, satisfied with the suggested pay of one coin (Matthew 20:2). As the day progressed, the vineyard owner hired more and more workers. At the end of the day, the men lined up to collect their pay. The hired men at 5 p.m. received payment of one coin. When the men hired early in the morning collected their pay, they were unsatisfied with the originally agreed-upon amount. They were jealous of the men who worked fewer hours and were blessed in the same capacity.

God uncomfortably exposed my similar sulky heart. I worked hard, sometimes suffering. I felt that I had earned a greater blessing. The vineyard owner addresses this attitude:

> *Friend, I am doing you no wrong. Did you*
> *not agree with me for a denarius? Take*

what belongs to you and go. I choose to
give to this last worker as I give to you.
Am I not allowed to do what I choose
with what belongs to me? Or do you
begrudge my generosity?

— MATTHEW 20:13-15

Jealousy bred discontent with the life God had chosen to give me. I needed to stop comparing myself with others and strive for contentment. Contentment comes from the Creator of the world, the giver of all good gifts, and as I started praising Him for His provision, my attitude shifted.

Having laundry to wash means we have clothes to wear. Having dishes to scrub means we have food to eat. Having bills to pay means we have a home and an income to support that home. Having a child to rear means we have the blessing of being parents. Every chore can be twisted into praise when viewed through the lens of blessing.

I started recording proof of God's provision. I gathered reminders of God's faithfulness, answered prayers, and goodness, and gave words to my faith. I journaled prayers, charted answers, told my friends how God was good, and asked them to remind me. I chose to believe in God's faithfulness and His sovereign character. It was a discipline to train my eyes to see His provision, to look for the blessing hiding behind each chore, to open my heart and pour out praise every day.

On slips of plain paper, I etched plain truth — one praise each day. It wasn't too much to make one acknowledgement of His goodness, mercy, and unchanging dependability. I stuffed these praises in a jar, my reminders that God is always good. My pile of stones gave witness to God's action.

God once instructed Joshua to order His people to build a pile of stones in their campsite. They were to use rocks taken from the river bed (Joshua 4:19-24).

This pile was to remind future generations how God's chosen people had safely crossed the Jordan River. My pile of stones reminds me that I've been here before. Waiting. Praying. Listening. It's my reminder that God always meets me in my moment of need. It's where I learned to be content with His choices for me. My story can encourage future generations to believe in His ability to meet every need. It is all for Him. Our hurt. Our scars. Our victories. Our gains. Our losses. Our brokenness. Even how and when He rebuilds us is not just about us. It is also about Him and is designed to point others toward Him if we let it. He is not worthy because of what He can do for us, but because of who He is. That, my dear sisters, must be enough.

This chapter is my story about wrestling down biblical contentment. It's also your story. What is that thing you believe will make you content? That thing is what you must wrestle down and leave on the altar.

But most importantly, this is God's story. My words are a drop in the ocean of letters scratched out for His glory across all time. God's words are the words that ultimately matter and will last for eternity. His words are living and became flesh. Christ, who is the Word, dwelt among us so that you and I could know and experience satisfaction in His perfect provision. In the world, we will have trouble, but we can take heart because Jesus has overcome this world (John 16:33). With Christ's help, we can live a life of thankfulness that boldly declares we are all for His glory.

PRAYER

*Lord, biblical contentment is not a feeling; it
is a choice. Help me choose to rejoice in
the goodness of You because my joy is
found in You, not my circumstances.
Lord, make my heart right with You
and help me rejoice in the radical work
You do through me for Your glory. My
life is Your life, and I am Your daughter.
Everything I own and everyone I love
belongs to You to do with as You see fit.
Lord, I surrender.*

— FOR YOUR GLORY

REFLECTION QUESTIONS

1. Have you ever felt forsaken by God or been broken by His answer of no? How did you respond?

2. Read Psalm 77. What is the psalmist's burden, and how did he find a resolution? How can you relate?

3. Is there bitterness in your heart that the Lord is calling you to lay before Him? What does replacing it with contentment look like?

4. How do you define biblical contentment? Is there such a thing as worldly contentment? Why or why not?

5. Rejoice and remember! Make a praise jar. Ask the Holy Spirit to help you praise the Lord for all His works in your life.

6. In what areas of your life has someone or
   something become the receiver of glory
   rather than God? What changes do you
   need to make to give this glory to God? How
   will you make that change?

Your Thoughts

Your Thoughts

_____

_____

_____

_____

_____

_____

_____

_____

_____

_____

_____

_____

_____

_____

_____

_____

_____

_____

_____

_____

_____

_____

Your Thoughts

7

PRAYER IS EVERYTHING

*S*ome days I am ashamed of my lack of desire for God, prayer, and intimacy with Him. I go through the motions of dutifully completing my routine of reading and studying Scripture, and yet my heart is already invested in what comes next—the busy schedule and tasks attached to the upcoming day. I can become so involved in pursuing and enjoying good activities that I fail to pursue the best goal—Him.

That leads me to wonder if I am really pursuing God or just pursuing His blessings? When I search my heart, will I find a love for Him or a love for what He can do for me? If He stripped His blessings away, would I continue to serve Him, pray to Him, and praise Him with joy because He is the gift? Would I grumble that my prayers for health or wealth went seemingly unanswered?

My heart twists uncomfortably under the microscope of questions that reveal my need for growth in prayer and dependence on God. There is a constant pushing and pulling within me. My spirit tugs me toward depth and intimacy with God, but the needs of the day push me away. This struggle is the battle between weak flesh and a longing spirit. I cannot win this battle on human strength.

We start by asking God to change our hearts and tug us closer to Him. We welcome the Holy Spirit and invite the painful process of exposing sin so that God can weed it out. It's messy, but it's beautiful. God will draw you closer and closer to Him, forcing you to examine why you come into His presence and why you don't. He tests our claim of being completely dependent on Him, claims which North American Christians easily spout while living in prosperity.

Why don't we pray more? Why do we rush to meet needs, give our opinion, and strive to fix things ourselves? These actions are all symptoms of a deeper and more worrisome problem. If we are not praying with passion and fervour or disciplining ourselves to pray during seasons that lack passion and fervour, then we must not believe or understand what Scripture says about prayer or the magnitude of its power. We have missed a valuable, theological truth—prayer matters.

An inflated sense of value is created when we disregard our sins of self-sufficiency, allowing housework, office work, hobbies, or leisure to consume hours meant for the Lord. If we prioritize picking up toys, wiping faces, and cleaning the clutter—yet fail to see the filth within our hearts—we minimize the raging battle between our flesh and His Spirit. The issue is not whether we have busy, full lives but that we wrongly believe our agendas are more important than prayer. The tasks of life have captured our time, attention, and hearts, and they have become more important than God.

Pastor Robbie Symons writes:

> Our actions prove that we do not believe in the power of prayer, or maybe more accurately, we believe more in the power of self.[1]
>
> — ROBBIE SYMONS - PASSION CRY

Our actions illustrate that we have greater faith in our ability to manage life than in the Creator of life. We value our wisdom above the Lord.

Prayerlessness is a symptom of sinful roots. When we allow comfort and schedules to slide into that sweet spot reserved only for God, it shoves Him and prayer down to second, third or fourth place in our lives. That is idolatry. It is bowing down to something else other than God (Exodus 20:3-5).

Lord, forgive us.

God is wise, infinite, sovereign, holy, all-knowing,

faithful, loving, all-powerful, self-existent, self-suffi-cient, just, never changing, merciful, eternal, good, gracious, everywhere. We have enough reason to praise Him—to roll out of bed and press our faces to the floor—because of who He is, not because of what we want Him to do.

We are sinful and broken women whose only hope for any future hinges entirely on the grace and mercy of God and the sacrifice His Son made for us.

A correct understanding of Him and His incompa-rably glorious nature and a proper understanding of self and our sinful, corruptible hearts should humble us to make our hearts right with God. It should humble us to seek forgiveness and transformation. Prayer has to be more than generating a bucket list of wants. The Holy Spirit moves in us through prayer and stirs our desire for more of God. He stirs our hearts for His word. He stirs our desire for a transformed life and repentance. It's simple and right.

> ... if my people who are called by my name humble themselves, and pray and seek my face and turn from their wicked ways, then I will hear from heaven and will forgive their sin and heal their land.
>
> — 2 CHRONICLES 7:14

If is a small word with a powerful impact. *If* places

a condition on God's promise. If we are called by His name ... What is the condition? That we belong to God. That we identify with Him. And more importantly, that He identifies with us. We do not belong to ourselves. We are His, bought with the blood of His Son. If we humble ourselves. We must get low and lift God high. We must admit our lack in contrast to His ability and declare a complete dependency on Him. If we pray, really pray. Real prayer is seeking Him and turning from the sin He reveals.

Then is another small word with a powerful impact. *If* places a condition on God's response. *Then* illustrates God's response to our obedience to the previous command. If I am called by God's name ... If I humble myself ... If I pray ... If I seek His face ... If I turn from sin ... *then* God answers. Then God forgives. Then God heals. Yet how often have we cried, wanting answers, healing, forgiveness, and blessings, but failed to stop our busyness and seek His face? Failed to heed the prompting of the Holy Spirit and turn from our sin? Failed to submit to Him and humble ourselves before Him? Failed to surrender whatever has slipped into God's place? How many times have we tried to tell God how His healing should look or what answer is best?

> *Oh Lord, You have said to seek Your face,*
> *and so Your face, Lord, we will seek. We*
> *have tasted and seen that You are good,*
> *but we long for more. You have not*

> *called us to try harder; you have called*
> *us to seek You. We must seek You first.*
> *In our humility and brokenness, we will*
> *lift our eyes to You. We repent. We have*
> *not loved You with our whole hearts.*
> *We repent that we have, at times, loved*
> *our status, things, lives and comforts*
> *more than You. This life is not ours. We*
> *must get low and lift You high. This life*
> *is not about us. We must love You more*
> *than we love ourselves.*
> *Open our eyes to the depths of our sins so*
> *we might love You more. Open our eyes*
> *to see where we have confused busyness*
> *with faithfulness.*
> *Forgive us.*

And we start here. Fresh. Dependent. Pliable. The depth of our prayer life reflects, in part, the depth of our love for the Lord. A deep prayer life doesn't need to sound fancy or go on for hours. It is raw, heartfelt, and real. It reveals our pure love for the Lord, and that love is displayed through time spent with Him and in His Word.

When we love God this much, we fervently protect that love and cultivate a reverence and awe of the Lord in our hearts. This reverence and awe is fear. We are not afraid; it's a respect based fear. It is a refusal to sink into flippancy in our relationship with Him.

66 The fear of the Lord is the beginning of wisdom and knowledge of the Holy One is insight.

— PROVERBS 9:10

Seeking human wisdom is like trying to quench our thirst for God from a dry well when He has invited us to drink from the well that never runs dry. Drinking deeply requires deep faith, which often requires deep reflection. We must learn to think deeply about the Lord.

Do we believe that deep intimacy with God matters? Will we do anything, give everything, and risk everything to find out? Until we desire to know God and love God with all our heart, soul, strength, and mind — regardless of the cost to ourselves — prayer might never find its rightful place in our lives.

Because reading a book about prayer is not the same as praying. Thinking about prayer is not the same as praying. Being concerned about the situation or need, or talking about a situation or need, is not the same as praying. Praying is praying.

You probably did not pray when you read this chapter, but you can pray right now. You can put this book down and confess the stirrings in your heart and ask God to reveal what has slipped into His place. You can stop reading the words penned by a woman and start reading God's Word. You can pray His Word back to Him with confidence that you are praying His will because when you pray His Word in the context it was written, you pray His will. You can stop trying to validate your feelings, to be understood, or to be right. Stop calling your girlfriends about every wound, worry, and need and instead commit to bringing those things to God first before anyone else. You can do it right now.

If we are not confessing our inability and expressing our faith in His ability, if we are not worshipping Him and surrendering our life, desires, and future to Him, then we are functioning on our strength, which cannot accomplish the kingdom work of introducing people to Jesus.

Prayer is our only defence against life's struggles and trials. It is the only way to keep moving forward in our faith, so we must ask the Lord to teach us how to pray. We wear His armor and wage war against the forces of darkness by His strength (Ephesians 6:10–18). Jesus is building His church, and the gates of hell will not prevail against it (Matthew 16:18).

PRAYER

I have tasted and seen that You are good,
*   but I long for more. I lift my eyes to You*
*   and repent of not loving You with my*
*   whole heart. I have loved my status,*
*   things, life, and comforts more than*
*   You. Open my eyes to the depth of my*
*   sins so I might love You more. Open my*
*   eyes to see where I have confused busy-*
*   ness with faithfulness. Forgive me.*
I pray, dear Lord, for a greater desire to
*   pray. Make me hunger and thirst know*
*   you more. Let nothing else satisfy.*
*   Show me your glory.*

— FOR YOUR GLORY

REFLECTION QUESTIONS

1. What captures your time in a day? Is prayer a priority?

2. What keeps you from better time management?

3. In chapter 2, question three, You set a one-month goal to spend time in the Word. Set a prayer goal to accompany this Scripture time.

4. How do you pray? What characterizes your prayers? Has your prayer life been reduced to a list of needs and requests?

5. Does your prayer life include adoration and worship of God? Make a list of all the reasons God is worthy of your praise. Now, pray through that list, thanking God for who He is.

6. Find a passage of Scripture that speaks to your current season of life and practice praying through Scripture. Try writing down your prayers, affirming what you learn about God's character as you study His Word.

Your Thoughts

Your Thoughts

_____

_____

_____

_____

_____

_____

_____

_____

_____

_____

_____

_____

_____

_____

_____

_____

_____

_____

_____

_____

_____

Your Thoughts

8

WHEN DARKNESS FALLS

*W*hen my husband and I stood at the precipice of ministry, I promised God I would follow Him no matter how overwhelming church life became. My young self had no idea how dark ministry could be. How lonely. How the arrows of the enemy are dipped in poison and meant to pierce deeply. When I purposely set my heart toward the Word of God, worship, prayer, and evangelism, the enemy's attacks increased. It left me very aware of my lack of training, ability, and experience. I remember the first time a rush of inadequacy washed over me. It was the first time I ached with a complete loss for words. I wanted to come alongside a woman nearly twice my age that was suffering greatly. What on earth could I offer of value? Every single word I considered speaking sounded trite and cold. At the naïve and childless age of 25, how could I understand what it meant to comfort and encourage a mother who had just lost her child? The time I spent training for ministry hadn't prepared me for this experience.

Over the years, this feeling fell over me again and again as I walked alongside women carrying heavy burdens. It hung like a suffocating cloak blocking out all light. In the ensuing darkness, I had to make a decision. Would I, as my husband would say, problem-solve through this person's pain in my wisdom? Would I retreat? Would I avoid the uncomfortable situation or person? Would this obstacle feed my fear or feed my faith?

Along with this feeling of inadequacy, darkness crept into my life in other ways. My husband faced physical illness. I suffered the emotional loss of infertility, failures, and spiritual attacks. There were many times when I didn't know what to do, but I knew I needed to do something. How would I get from where I was to where I needed to be?

Maybe you've felt similar emotions. Maybe you've known the overwhelming feelings of inadequacies and failure. In those moments, we need God's wisdom to face the issue and not flee the scene. We need His strength to declare our dependence on Him. Instead of falling to defeat, we can fall to our knees. We can come before the Lord and admit that we don't understand His plan, but we recognize that if anything changes for the good, it will come through Him. This is humility. Humility drives us to seek God over our needs and cling to Him. Humility prompts a heart-check, an examination to see if we are in the faith.

My ministry position running successful programs and my marriage to a pastor doesn't guarantee that my heart is right before God because salvation is not earned through works. Good works are the overflow of a heart that's right with God. We do not find joy, hope, and peace from worldly success, a perfect family, a cushy bank account, or a cozy house. We will not find lasting joy from human accomplishments and reaching lofty goals. It is found only in Christ.

Our eyes must be fixed on God. When evil steals all the security this world has to offer and the best doctor has no hope, when the bank account is empty, when the illness is fatal, or the accident is life-changing, our eyes must be fixed on the Light—set on the unchanging security found in a right relationship with God.

We cannot fix our eyes on the temporary or fearsome shadows that seek to cover the light. We set our eyes on Jesus. He scatters the darkness. The night is as bright as the day because He is the light. He holds us. His right hand guides us. When evil presses in, He lifts our heads and fixes our gaze upon Him. He's inescapable. He never lets us go. He is God.

Don't give in to the darkness. Act on the faith you might not always feel but believe and know to be true. Believe in the God who loves you, saves you and hears your prayers. Will your physical, emotional, and spiritual challenges feed your fear or feed your faith?

I longed for the joy of complete dependence on God yet feared the cost of full surrender. I longed for unconditional acceptance and love but feared exposing my heart. I longed for the solid piece that comes with absolute trust and contentment amidst alarming circumstances but feared those alarming circumstances might shatter my soul. How do I starve my fear and feed my faith? In overwhelming inadequacies, how do I believe that God is enough and that He will provide?

This paradox of deep desire and dark worry is a dance of continual surrender. It is a cycle of acknowledging my fears and choosing to trust God in the midst of them. It is a cycle of admitting that I don't know the answers, but if my eyes are fixed on the One who does, I'll be okay. The only response to fear is to trust in God more.

Tough, dark times challenged the truths I embraced in the light of good times. The dark moments of being unable to have biological children, facing ministry opposition, spiritual attacks, and tremendous grief, coping when friends failed, and when I failed, all whispered that God couldn't work through a person like me. I should give up.

These tough, dark times skilfully wove half-truths with lies. I was failing in many ways. I couldn't fix anything on my own. I don't have anything to offer in my strength. However, praise God that this inadequacy can all be overcome through the power of His Holy Spirit. God has made a way for me to enjoy and celebrate family. He's paved a way of victory through spiritual opposition and attack. He granted me the humility to seek forgiveness and extend grace. He worked through my sinful self and accomplished great things for His kingdom. His strength in me will endure. He has brought me to the place where I can look back over these trials and see His hand guiding me. I see His protection in the tragic, His provision in the need. In those trials, He proved to me that He is all that I have to offer anyone. And He is more than enough.

What do I tell a grieving mother? A widowed spouse? A victim of a violent attack? Trite and easy answers do not satisfy when God's goodness is at stake. Truth proclaims that our God is good in darkness and light, when it is easy and hard, when He gives and when He takes away. There is no room for a feel-good prosperity gospel that fails to recognize the cost and sacrifice of a fully surrendered heart to Christ in a broken world.

I tell them what I tell myself. Fix your eyes on Jesus. Echo the beautiful prayer of Jehoshaphat in 2 Chronicles 20:12:

> ❝ ... We do not know what to do, but our eyes are on You.

No matter how far the enemy twists the dimmer, one Light will not be extinguished. That holy Light descends into our shadowy world to open our eyes. We fix our eyes on Him. We do not know why God doesn't act when He can or why He allows heartbreak and hurt, except to say that Scripture foretells the future of this broken earth and says that the path to glory is going to be wrought with hardship.

> Lord, we don't know what to do, but our
> eyes are fixed on You. They are fixed on
> the Way, the Truth, and the Life. To live
> is Christ. To die is gain. Blessed be the
> name of the Lord.

This world is not our home. This world will disappoint. Our ministry will hurt. Our friends may let us down. Our hearts may break. Our bodies will fail. One day we will exhale our last breath of the temporary and inhale eternity.

Our whole being should ache for the fulfilment of the promise of peace in a place filled with pure joy and devoid of tears. We should ache for this broken world that is a dim shadow of the glory to come. We should ask for the promise of newness under our Lord and Saviour's ruling because we do not belong in this world. This world is not our home. We must shift our eyes from the temporary and fix them on the eternal.

While we wait for that glorious day when all wrongs are made right, the darkness will deepen. Some days everything will fall off the rails or look as if it is about to, and we won't know where to begin picking up the pieces.

On those dark and difficult days, humble yourself and pray. Fix your eyes on the Lord and cling to His Word. He will change the way you view your circumstances and the solutions you seek. Our focus ceases to be about being right, proving ourselves, obtaining success, or getting our way. Our focus centres on deflecting all glory to God, where it belongs.

One day the children of God will be ushered away from the presence of those we could never imagine leaving and into the presence of the One who never leaves. Will be home and proclaim that it was worth it all.

While shrouded in this present darkness, we cannot imagine the glowing, triumphant welcome that awaits us on the other side. The indescribable love, laughter, and joy as mortality puts on in mortality and enters into eternity with the Lord.

While we wait for this glorious homecoming, we blink. We blink back hurt, grief, and a longing for what this world cannot provide. Pain, although sharp and deep, is a sweet reminder that we are only visitors on earth. Our family and the ministries and talents entrusted to us are only on loan from the One who owns it all. The One who, we pray, will one day look upon us with love and joy, declaring, "Well done good and faithful servant" (Matthew 25:23).

One day, we will open our eyes in the place where victory swallows death. We will meet our Saviour face-to-face and know that we are home. We will praise Him with an eternal perspective. We will know it was all worth His glory.

PRAYER

Lord, I don't know what to do, but my eyes are fixed on You. They are set on the Way, the Truth, and the Life. To live is Christ. To die is gain. Blessed be the name of the Lord.

— FOR YOUR GLORY

REFLECTION QUESTIONS

1. What does the Bible have to say about humility? Find several verses and write them down.

2. Scripture encourages us to examine ourselves and see if we are in the faith (2 Corinthians 13:5). Read the short letter of 1 John and examine your faith.

3. What does Matthew 7:20 say about a believer? What happens to fruitless branches (John 15:2)? How does Galatians 5:22–23 describe fruit?

4. What do the following verses say about fear? 1 John 4:18, Isaiah 41:10, Matthew 10:28-31, and Psalm 56:3.

5. How does time spent in the Word feed our faith? See Psalm 119:103-105.

6. Why are good works important if they can't save us? See James 2:14-17, Matthew 5:16, Colossians 3:23-24, Hebrews 13:6.

7. Praise the Lord that you are not the answer to your problem; God is! Petition the Lord for the next several days to reveal how the Holy Spirit is at work in your life to free you from darkness and enjoy and celebrate freedom. Make a list of what you learn.

8. Meditate on God's promise of eternity with Him.

Your Thoughts

CHASED BY GRACE · CHANGED BY LOVE

Your Thoughts

_____

_____

_____

_____

_____

_____

_____

_____

_____

_____

_____

_____

_____

_____

_____

_____

_____

_____

_____

_____

_____

_____

Your Thoughts

9

GRACE COVERS IT ALL

race matters. The grace that saves us from our sin is the same grace that keeps us until the end. God's grace is what makes the kind of surrender we explored in this book possible, the type of surrender that I believe God requires. This grace should radically impact us because grace is the unmerited favour of God. Unmerited means undeserved. We can never earn it. It flies in the face of our culture where everything is based on merit. A solid academic performance earns good grades. A job completed earns a salary. But God's grace is unmerited. We cannot work for it; we work because of it.

According to Isaiah 66:2, something must be true in our hearts for God to look our way:

>> ...But this is the one to whom I (the Lord) will look: he who is humble and contrite in spirit and trembles at my word.

Humble and contrite. From cover to cover, the Bible tells us that grace is unmerited, and those who genuinely understand grace realize they don't deserve it and accept it through a humble and contrite heart. Because of grace, we have the undeserved attention of God as He turns toward us. God turns. God initiates it. He turns toward us, and we see the grace of God in the fullness of Jesus Christ (Titus 2:11). His grace comes down. Jesus came down to us. Our praise and thanks rise in return, and God's glory goes out.

We're at the end of a book on surrender, and there is much to yield. Perhaps you don't know where to begin. Everything you once claimed as yours has been revealed as originating and belonging to God for His glory. Settling that truth is paramount to moving forward with a proper heart because it is much easier to give back to God something we've determined belongs to Him first.

Yet, our fingers instinctively tighten. What if it hurts? What if He takes it? What if life becomes uncomfortable? What if we embraced His grace? All truth with no grace generates helplessness, hopelessness and weighty, unrelenting guilt. All grace and no truth produces a life without boundaries. But praise God; after exposing us to His truth, He sends down grace that covers it all, so when the roots of our sin run deep, His grace increases.

> What shall we say then? Are we to continue in sin that grace may abound? By no means! How can we who died to sin still live in it?
>
> — ROMANS 6:1–2

To be the doers of the Word that God has called us to become, to live victorious lives not dependent on pleasing circumstances, to fill the role He has crafted us to fill, to keep Him in the number one place in our hearts, we need the saving power of the cross. This is God's greatest grace to us.

His grace enables us to fulfill the highest calling on our lives to exalt Him. His grace gives us new mercies every morning. His grace provides us with the ability and desire to surrender. His grace heals all our hurts in His timing. His grace comes down, unleashing our praise that declares that these difficulties are for His glory.

Jesus understands hard surrender. There was nothing easy about His death on the cross. There was nothing easy about the beatings, ridicule, pierced flesh, or torn skin. He knew what awaited Him; still, He did more than simply yield to God's will; He moved toward it, reaching out a loving hand to heal those who persecuted Him (Luke 22:51). He loved His enemies right to the end. But, it wasn't really an end; it was a beginning.

By God's grace, the cross tells His message of love. Suffering will come to followers of Christ purely because we follow Christ. Jesus' trek to the cross confirms that He understands life is difficult when we surrender to God's will. The mess at the cross—the beatings, blood, death of Christ—displays God's glory. My husband explains it like this:

> Christ's death led to His exultation when He was raised in new life by the power of the Father. He now sits at God's right hand and makes intercession for you and me. That means it was never over at the cross, and His grace to us assures us that if we identify with Jesus and it leads to hardship, it is never over for us.
>
> — KEVIN WEEKS

Suffering shows God's resurrection power as God works through our surrendered hearts and proves it is never over with Him. God is using the most challenging things in our lives to prepare us to stand before Him. The glory we will one day experience is so out of proportion to the suffering we may now endure.

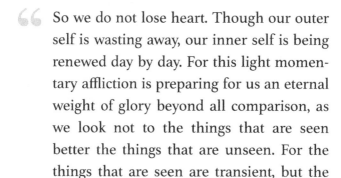

So we do not lose heart. Though our outer self is wasting away, our inner self is being renewed day by day. For this light momentary affliction is preparing for us an eternal weight of glory beyond all comparison, as we look not to the things that are seen better the things that are unseen. For the things that are seen are transient, but the things that are unseen are eternal.

— 2 CORINTHIANS 4:16–18

Afflictions are only light when we compare them with what awaits in glory. Compare your trial. Test the Scripture, and you will see that God's grace for you is the promise of glory. There is nothing we can surrender here that we will regret in eternity. So surrender. Die to self and embrace the grace of God's resurrection power. Transformation happens in that place of total surrender. By God's power, your life ceases to conform to the world and is transformed with a renewed mind that no longer desires to satisfy self as much as it desires to glorify God through bearing fruit in every good work. We don't work for the transformation; we work because of it (Colossians 1:10). God's grace is a coming day when we will be ushered into His presence, and all pain will cease.

But until then, clay pots break. We are weak, feeble vessels made of clay who break under the pressure of life to show "the surpassing power belongs to God" (2 Corinthians 4:7). It is when the vessel breaks that the treasure of Jesus can pour out.

> We are afflicted in every way, but not crushed; perplexed, but not driven to despair; persecuted, but not forsaken; struck down, but not destroyed; always carrying in the body the death of Jesus, so that the life of Jesus may also be manifested in our bodies.
>
> — 2 CORINTHIANS 4:8 –10

Jesus pours out of our brokenness and covers our mess with His grace because the surpassing power belongs to God. That power supports a freeing truth. If we place our trust in Jesus Christ and His payment for our sin, God already loves us as much as He possibly can. Our obedience does not earn more love, and disobedience doesn't remove His love. It's unmerited. God already loves us and sees us through the lens of Christ. Our covenant-keeping Lord always, always, always keeps His promises to His people. His grace is enough because He says it is (2 Corinthians 12:9).

I pray that you won't remember a message of the guilt from this book, but rather that you would feel conviction and understand that conviction is not condemnation. Conviction comes from the Holy Spirit

(John 16:8) and prompts genuine repentance. Romans 8:1 states that "there is therefore now no condemnation for those who are in Christ Jesus." The law no longer has the power to condemn us because Jesus perfectly fulfilled the law, and believers are "in Christ" (Romans 8:3).

God's grace for you is the conviction that you can no longer linger in disobedience or mediocrity in a tepid, lukewarm faith. God's grace pursues you, as He pursued me, never giving up and never letting us give up. He increases the weight we carry until we lay it at His feet. God's grace for you is a fresh inability to settle for complacency in that comfortable spot where faith costs you little. God's grace is calling you from rules and obligatory actions to a passionate pursuit of Him. His grace is calling you to move toward Him in full surrender and embrace His unrelenting love that continually refines and changes you until you are more like Jesus. His grace came down. His grace is the beauty hidden in the broken. His grace abounds in messy lives. His grace opens your eyes to see that it was less about you and more about Him. His grace enables you to leave your most significant, most profound, and most painful experiences with Him to do with as He sees fit. His grace breaks down walls — walls between Him and us and walls between us and others. His grace is supernatural contentment amid ever-changing circumstances. His grace is passionate prayers that expose the idols that have crept into the place reserved only for God. His grace is a truth that explodes in the darkness, shedding light into every corner of the heart. He is calling each one of us to choose between our way and His way. His grace has come down. It's time to respond for His glory.

PRAYER

You already love me as much as You
possibly can because I've placed my
trust in the blood of Jesus Christ for
payment of my sin. You love me, and
You see me through the lens of Christ.
Your loving kindness leads me to
repentance.
I will no longer linger in disobedience or in a
lukewarm faith. I don't want to stay in
a where faith costs me so little. You are
calling me out from the rules of oblig-
atory actions into a passionate pursuit
of You. Your unrelenting love is refining
and changing me, making me more like
Jesus.

— FOR YOUR GLORY

PERSONAL REFLECTION

We are at the end of our journey together, but you and the Lord have further to go. Starting today, and for the following four weeks, I've provided Scripture passages and questions to work through. Don't rush these exercises. Invite the Holy Spirit to refine you and teach you.

I recommend working through one set of questions each week. I've spent much of the last few years in these passages, and they have comforted and challenged my heart. I pray that they will do the same for you.

2 Chronicles 20:1-30

It's easy to feel anxious about the unknown future, government overreach, health concerns, financial need or many other issues. Hardships and uncertainty are real concerns. Work through the following questions to learn from King Jehoshaphat how to respond in moments of fear.

Read 2 Chronicles 20:1-30

1. Think of the last time you felt fear. Your fear could be connected to a specific circumstance or event or it can be more general in nature. Either way, fear rouses a response in us. How did you respond to your fear? List the ways.

2. Compare and contrast how you responded to your fear with how King Jehoshaphat responded to his fear in 2 Chronicles 20:1-21.

3. King Jehoshaphat's prayer is found in verses 6-12. There are five shifts of focus in this prayer. Title each one of the five sections of prayer according to the focus of those verses:

- Verse 6:
- Verse 7:
- Verses 8-9:
- Verses 10-11:
- Verse 12:

Answered Prayers and Commands

1. How does King Jehoshaphat's prayer show that he approached God with a humble heart? According to James 4:6 & 10, why is humility before God necessary?

2. God answers Jehoshaphat's prayer through Jahaziel (v15-17). God gives the people one command in verse 15, another command in verse 16, three commands in verse 17a, and then repeats two commands that were earlier stated in verse 17b. List all the commands God gives the people in the space below. According to your observations, to whom does the battle belong, and therefore, who declares to fight the battle, and why does that matter (v15, 17)?

- (v15)
- (v16)
- (v17a)
- (v17a)
- (v17a)
- (v17b)
- (v17b)

A commentary on 2 Chronicles writes 2 Chronicles 20:15, 17 and Exodus 14:13-14 are the only two passages in all of Scripture that combines the phrases *do not be afraid*, *take your stand*, and *see the Lord's deliverance*.[1] In both instances, the people were required to respond in faith.

1. What action illustrated the Israelites faith in God in Exodus 14? In general, how would you describe their attitude toward God's anticipated provision?

2. What action illustrated Judah's faith in God in 2 Chronicles 20? In general, how would you describe their attitude toward God's anticipated provision?

3. What do your actions illustrate regarding your faith or lack of faith in God? What does your attitude say about you?

4. How did Jehoshaphat instruct the people in verse 20?

5. What would it look like for you to put your trust in God? What could enduring and succeeding look like in your current battle?

6. God acted on behalf of His people as they worshipped Him in singing and praising. What did the people of Judah do?

7. What does it look like to worship your way through your current battle? How can you

cultivate this attitude of worship in your heart? List specific actions you can take.

God fought for His people and gave the people of Judah victory, spoils of a war they did not fight, and peace (v22-30).

1. According to Galatians 5:17, Ephesians 6:11-12, 1 Peter 2:11 and 5:8, and James 1:13-15, what is our greatest battle? Who is it against? What is at stake?
2. How does God secure our victory in this battle? See 1 Corinthians 15:57, 1 Peter 2:24, Colossians 2:13-15.
3. What blessings are ours to claim as a result of God's victory? See 2 Corinthians 4:17-18, Ephesians 1:3-13, 2:8-9, James 1:12.

Application:

Follow Jehoshaphat's prayer from verses 6-12 and write out a prayer to God regarding your current struggle or fear. This prayer begins with who God is, remembers what God has done, recalls how you've responded to God in the past, presents the current problem, and declares God is the solution and resolves to act accordingly. Be specific, and remember the importance of approaching God with a humble heart!

God, You are ...

God, I remember the ways You have ...

In the past, I have responded in/with ...

Right now, I am facing <battle/fear> ...

God, I declare that I believe that You are the solution! Because of this, I will ...

Your Thoughts

Your Thoughts

Your Thoughts

10

MARK 5:21-43

I love stories because, as a novelist, I love the emotional climb toward a black moment when all hope is lost. I love journeying with characters into disasters that force them to make impossible decisions. I love how a good author ties up the story threads in a satisfying way.

Today's narrative passage has a similar story pattern, but the difference is that these people are not characters. Jairus was a real man, with a real daughter, with a real need. The bleeding woman was a real woman, judged by society and desperate for hope. But like well-written stories and novels, these real people were forced to make a decision in their crisis moments. They risked everything to reach this moment. Will they fall prey to their fears? Or, will they find the courage to reach out for Jesus?

Read Mark 5:21-43

1. Tell about a time you needed someone's help, but you feared the answer might be no.

2. Narratives contain a story arc. There is a **beginning**, which introduces the characters and sets the scene. **Rising action** increases the tension. A **climax** is when all hope seems lost and a decision is made. **Falling action** answers the story questions and begins to resolve the story problem. The **resolution** occurs when the story problem has been answered, and a new setting or a change in story direction occurs. Keeping this format in mind, create two story arcs that includes Scripture references, one for Jairus and one for the bleeding woman. All verses pertaining to each narrative must be on the arc. (Hint: the bleeding woman's story has its narrative arc AND has a place on Jairus' narrative arc.)

3. Compare and contrast Jairus (v21-24, 35-43) and the bleeding woman (v25-34). How are their needs, their social standing, and their circumstances similar? How are they different?

4. With which needs do you most resonate? Why?

5. How do Jairus' humble actions in verses 22-23 illustrate how you should approach God with your needs?

6. What does the placement of the bleeding woman's story within Jairus' narrative reveal about the character of Jesus?

7. Read Leviticus 15:19-23. In light of that passage, why do you suppose the bleeding woman hid in the crowd and attempted to sneak healing from Jesus (v27-30)?

8. Continue reading Leviticus 15:24-33. For what reasons could Jesus have had for calling attention to the touch and healing of the bleeding woman (v31-35)?

9. What is the significance of Jesus calling the woman "daughter" in verse 34? How was she referenced earlier in the chapter (v25, 33)? What was required of her to become a daughter (v33-34)?

10. According to John 1:12-13, how does one become a "daughter" of God?

11. What evidences exist in your life that prove a relationship or lack of relationship with God?

12. Both Jairus and the woman took their need to Jesus, but Mark notes the woman brought her need after her attempts to fix

her problem had failed. What are some of the ways we attempt fixing our problems?

13. What lies do you believe that cause you to wait so long to bring your problems to Jesus?

14. List the current needs in your life and rate them in importance. 1 being the most significant need and 5 being the least.

15. What changes in your life could ensure you have enough time and emotional energy to bring your number one concern before the Lord?

16. In light of the instructions listed in Leviticus 22:4-6, why does it astonish that Jesus took Jairus' daughter by the hand (v41)?

17. What specific instructions is Jairus given in verse 36? What choices did he have at that moment? What were the results of his choices (v41-42)?

18. What might God be trying to sift in your heart in light of your current trials and suffering? What would it look like to bring these needs to Jesus and how will you rest in Him as you wait for His provision?

Remember:

The interruption of the bleeding woman moves forward the central message of the story: the antidote to fear is faith. Nothing—not even death—can stop Christ from accomplishing His purposes in your life. We must have faith in Him (Mark 5:34, 36).

The physical healing of the bleeding woman and the dead girl points toward our need for spiritual healing. The law dictated that anyone who touched an unclean person would be made unclean, but when Jesus—who is the perfect fulfillment of the law (Matt 5:17-20)—touched them, He imparted His cleanliness (2 Cor 5:21) establishing His authority as God.

We are the unclean woman shunned by society and desperate. We are the girl dead in our sins and without hope. We are Jairus desperate for God's intervention. When Jesus intervenes and touches us, when we respond to Him in repentant and obedient faith, we gain new life and are made clean.

Your Thoughts

Your Thoughts

_____

_____

_____

_____

_____

_____

_____

_____

_____

_____

_____

_____

_____

_____

_____

_____

_____

_____

_____

_____

_____

Your Thoughts

_____

_____

_____

_____

_____

_____

_____

_____

_____

_____

_____

_____

_____

_____

_____

_____

_____

_____

_____

_____

_____

_____

11

PSALM 77

The children of God have a choice to make. We can press into God and His Word and fight against fear with the truth that never changes, or we can succumb to dread and anxiety. I am choosing to fill my mind with the Word of God.

If you join me in Psalm 77, you'll find some striking similarities between the psalmist and us. The people of God are in distress, and the psalmist cries out to God. He is in a moment like ours, and he decides to turn his attention and energy toward prayer and meditation. If you follow along with the psalmist, you'll find that God leads his people through by the hand. I don't know about you, but I can't think of a better place to be right now than hand-in-hand with God.

Read Psalm 77

1. In verses 3, 6, and 11-12, the psalmist repeats his decision to do two things. What has the psalmist decided to do?

2. Consider the progression of his decision preceded by the words when (v3), let me (v6), and I will (v11-12). What do these words convey about biblical thinking?

3. In verses 1-9, the focus in on the psalmist. If you mark every reference to the psalmist and then every reference to the Lord, you will notice a 20:12 ratio. The psalmist is very focused on himself. In verses 10-15, this begins to shift—the ratio changes to 7:15 in favour of the Lord. Finally, in verses 16-20, the entire focus is the Lord. Ten times the Lord is referenced, ending with a declaration in verse 19-20. What does the psalmist declare?

4. In verse 19, the word *through* shows the relationship between *way* and *sea*. The same word *through* shows the relationship between *path* and *water*. What is the significance of the word through? How might this apply to your struggles?

5. It is frightening to consider what going through hardship might mean for us.

What comfort can you find in the last half of verse 19? What is the significance of the word unseen, and how does it comfort you today?

6. In what two ways does God lead His people in verse 20? Explain what those phrases meant for the psalmist and what they mean for you today.

Pray:

> *Lord, I need you. When I am troubled, help me to remember Your goodness, love, and kindness toward me. Help me to ponder Your work and meditate on Your mighty deeds. When I am tempted to fear, bring to my mind the ways You have delivered Your people in the past. When I long to detour around the hardship that You are leading me through, remind me that You are with me. Put a song of praise in my heart that I can sing through the darkest night. We walk together. You lead me by the hand. There is no safer place to be.*
>
> *Amen*

Your Thoughts

Your Thoughts

_____

_____

_____

_____

_____

_____

_____

_____

_____

_____

_____

_____

_____

_____

_____

_____

_____

_____

_____

Your Thoughts

_____

_____

_____

_____

_____

_____

_____

_____

_____

_____

_____

_____

_____

_____

_____

_____

_____

_____

_____

_____

_____

_____

12

ROMANS 8:18-30

*E*veryone suffers. So, the question is not will we suffer. The question is will we suffer well? God has a purpose in suffering; we only need to look to the suffering of Christ as evidence. The suffering of Christ was an event that God did not merely allow but had ordained for His sovereign purposes to bring about the salvation and restoration of all creation, something the people could not see clearly at that time. Before beginning the questions below, pray for the Holy Spirit to enable you to view your suffering through the lens of God working out a greater purpose that you might not understand but trust to be for your ultimate good.

Read Romans 8:18-30

1. What are some ways suffering exists or presents in the world?

2. The author compares two things in verse 18. What conclusion does he make regarding that comparison?

3. Is the phrase "is to be revealed" written in the past, present, or future tense? How should the tense of that phrase impact the way we view our suffering?

4. How does verse 19 and 23 describe creation as it waits for the revealing of the sons of God and how we wait for adoption and the redemption of our bodies? What image does that description stir in your mind?

5. Some of us are waiting to reach milestones such as graduation, marriage, having a family, or obtaining a dream career. Some of us are waiting for good news or for circumstances to change. List the things for which you are eagerly waiting.

6. Alongside this feeling of eager anticipation, the author writes that both creation and people groan inwardly (v22-23). Suffering can be a result of personal sin, the result of being sinned against, attacks from the

enemy, or the results of living in a fallen world. In question one, you considered suffering in a broader sense. Keeping in mind the theology of suffering and how God works through suffering, from where does your suffering originate?

7. Hope is mentioned five times in verses 24-25. The Spirit is mentioned four times in verses 26-27. What is the Spirit's role in bringing hope to the believer? What comfort does this bring you?

8. Verse 28a is a beautiful reminder that God works all things together for those who love Him. According to verses 28-30, God acts on the believer's behalf. What has God done in the past, what does He do now, and what will He do in the future for those called according to His purpose?

Pray:

> *Lord, I believe that nothing will separate me from Your love. Not tribulation, distress, persecution, need, danger, or sword. Neither death, nor life, angels nor rulers, things present nor things to come, powers, height, depth, nor*

*anything else in all creation will be able
to separate me from Your love. I know
this in my head. Help me to believe this
in my heart.*

Amen.

Your Thoughts

_____

_____

_____

_____

_____

_____

_____

_____

_____

_____

_____

_____

_____

_____

_____

_____

_____

_____

_____

_____

Your Thoughts

_____

_____

_____

_____

_____

_____

_____

_____

_____

_____

_____

_____

_____

_____

_____

_____

_____

_____

_____

_____

_____

_____

Your Thoughts

13

PSALM 13

*H*ow long will we fight these same battles? How long will chaos and turmoil abound in the streets? News report after news report lands heavily on my heart. Has God forgotten us? Has He turned away from us? Sorrow lingers all day. How long until God intervenes? How long until relief?

Some fights will continue until the Lord returns or takes us home. We fight for the truth. We fight for sanity. We fight for justice. It's equally vital that we fight against the falling curtain of despair or encroaching fears. It is easy to get stuck in the lingering sorrow, anguish, and despair, but this is not a safe place to remain. Join me in Psalm 13 and acknowledge your woes, declare your dependence on the Lord, and resolve to take the only action that can change your heart. Work through Psalm 13 and feel every emotion the psalmist expresses in those early verses, and then determine to follow his example in the end.

Read Psalm 13

1. When have you felt forgotten, unseen, or not important enough? Create a list of words that describe how you felt at that moment.

2. Many of the words on your list could likely be used to describe the psalmist's emotional state in verses 1-2. The psalmist asks the Lord four questions in his grief (1-2). When we are overwhelmed, it is common to ask questions. What questions do you have for the Lord pertaining to your current needs and concerns?

3. It's doubtful the psalmist expected answers from God. Asking his questions was more likely a way of communicating his anguish on feeling forgotten. Read Isaiah 44:21 and 49:15. What do these verses indicate about God's memory?

4. Based on what you've learned from Isaiah 44:21 and 49:15, it's clear that the psalmist's feelings of being forgotten are not a reliable source of truth. How do your feelings in emotionally charged moments threaten to

lead you astray? Find at least one truth from Scripture that can speak into those lies.

5. Psalm 13 shifts in verses 3 and 4. The psalmist stops expressing his sorrow and begins asking the Lord to intervene. What are the possible results of the Lord failing to intervene in the psalmist's life (4)?

6. How do you need the Lord to intervene in your life? What do you fear might happen if the Lord does not intervene?

7. Another shift occurs in verse 5 indicated by the word "but," which contrasts all the earlier despair with decisions the psalmist has made. What three things does the psalmist resolve to do (5-6a)?

8. What do you learn about God's character from verse 5-6a?

9. Why does the psalmist decide to do these things (6b)?

10. The NASB, ESV, NKJV and the KJV all use the word "bountifully" in verse 6. What images does the word bountiful bring to your mind? Make a list of synonyms for the word bountiful.

11. Where else in Scripture do we see God dealing with His people and expressing His love for His people in lavish and bountiful ways?

12. How has the Lord "dealt bountifully" with you?

13. Jesus understands what it is like to feel far from God. What does He say in Matthew 27:46 and Mark 15:34 that conveys the agony of His soul? Also, see Hebrews 5:7. What does Christ's suffering as a punishment for our sins reveal about God's love for us? What sort of response does that stir in you?

Application

Go back to your answer for question eight and praise the Lord for His character qualities that never change.

Rejoice in your salvation (5a).

Praise the Lord in song (6a). Either sing, listen to, or sing along with a worship song that expresses your trust in the Lord.

Confess the fears you have listed in question six and express your trust in the Lord to work in those circumstances (5).

Thank the Lord for His kindness and mercy toward you that you discovered answering questions ten through thirteen.

Your Thoughts

Your Thoughts

_____

_____

_____

_____

_____

_____

_____

_____

_____

_____

_____

_____

_____

_____

_____

_____

_____

_____

_____

_____

Your Thoughts

_____

_____

_____

_____

_____

_____

_____

_____

_____

_____

_____

_____

_____

_____

_____

_____

_____

_____

_____

_____

_____

_____

NOTES

1. Broken Beautifully

1. C.S. Lewis, The Lion, the Witch, and the Wardrobe (London, UK: Geoffrey Bles, 1950).

7. Prayer is Everything

1. Robbie Symons, Passion Cry (Winnipeg, MB: Word Alive Press, 2016), 108.

Personal Reflection

1. Selman, M. J. (1994). *2 Chronicles: an introduction and commentary* (Vol. II, p. 446). Downers Grove, IL: InterVarsity Press.

ACKNOWLEDGMENTS

~

Writing is never a one-person adventure. Despite the hours I live inside my head working on a story or book, countless others invest in the project. Pastors Kevin, Robbie, Todd and Norm have encouraged me more than words can say. Thank you.

I would have never ventured into the second edition of Glorious Surrender without the encouragement of my writing friends in the Brantford Writers Group. Thank you, Karen, Sandy, Heather, and Tara, for your enthusiasm and belief in me.

A special thanks to the many authors who answered my questions and calmed my fears about publishing. The author community is the best!

ABOUT THE AUTHOR

Stacey is a ministry wife, mother of three teenagers, and a sipper of hot tea with honey. She loves to open the Word of God and share the hope of Christ with women. She is a multi-award-winning author, the primary home-educator of her children, and a frequent conference speaker. Her messages have been described as rich in the truths of Scripture, gospel-infused, and life-changing. Stacey has a Graduate Certificate in Women's Ministry with Heritage College and Seminary and is working toward a Graduate Certificate in Biblical Counselling.

MAKE A DIFFERENCE
PLEASE REVIEW GLORIOUS SURRENDER

Did you enjoy this book? You can make a difference. Honest reviews of books bring them to the attention of other readers. If you enjoyed this book, I would be grateful if you could spend a few minutes to leave an online review.

ALSO BY STACEY WEEKS

Chasing Holiness

For your next study, order Chasing Holiness and spend seven weeks learning how to live by the power of God and cultivate a lifestyle in keeping with who you really are in Christ.

"In a day of 'hamster wheel,' chaotic lives in pursuit of the temporal, the call to chase after holiness is joyfully welcomed."
Robbie Symons, Author of *Passion Cry*

Chasing
Holiness
A Seven-Week Study

Train for the Race
You are Already
Running

Stacey Weeks

We all chase something. It might be a degree or career, a husband and family, the approval of man, or a perception of social success. We long to pursue the things that matter, we long to chase the Lord, but we are weary. What would happen if we redirected our energy toward developing the character traits and disciplines that Christ calls us to pursue? What if we sought ways to increase our endurance and strengthen our faith? What if we stopped aimlessly running and instead chased the disciplines that would earn the prize that mattered? Chasing Holiness challenges the status quo level of Christian living accepted for far too long by many women today. It's about teaching stubborn hearts through the discipline of seeking God to remain focused on Him. It examines what it means to live by the power of God and believe Him when He calls us a daughter, chosen, holy, and redeemed. It encourages women to cultivate a lifestyle in keeping with who we really are in Christ. It's an acknowledgment that many of us long to fix our eyes on Jesus and push toward the finish line, but we don't know where to start. Chasing Holiness is about finding out together.

Praise for Chasing Holiness

"Stacey style of writing guides the not-yet believer gently, informs the recent believer, and challenges the mature believer toward the desire for all Christians — holiness. Themes of doctrine, Scripture, and day-to-day life with its struggles are presented as understandable and relatable to the reader. One isn't left feeling inadequate but rather inspired to chase after holiness as a result of reading this work."

— LAURA COLWELL - DIRECTOR OF WOMEN'S MINISTRY, HOPE BIBLE CHURCH, OAKVILLE ONTARIO

"I want every woman in our church to read and study *Chasing Holiness*. There is nothing easy about Stacey's words. This is a clear and necessary call to holy living. A call that is sadly absent from many pulpits and "Christian" books today. With honesty and transparency, Stacey shares from her own life but not in that I've-got-it-all-figured-out kind of way. The reader will feel the connection and be moved into the chase with her. The book is saturated with Scripture, moving from powerful explanations of the biblical texts to application that is simple and accessible. The study questions at the end of each chapter, Bible study group plan, and list of additional resources make this a must-have book for women who are serious about their walk with Christ."

— TODD DUGARD, LEAD PASTOR - HARVEST BIBLE CHAPEL, BARRIE ONTARIO

"Foundational to Christian living is a proper knowledge of God and responding submissively and completely. This study blends biblical insight with practical reflection to help move us forward in our intimacy with Jesus."

— ANDREA THOM - BIBLE TEACHER, AUTHOR OF RUTH: REDEEMING THE DARKNESS AND AMOS: COME AWAKE

"Stacey Weeks accurately identifies a massively concerning issue in today's church culture. We long for Jesus but we risk missing Him all together. This is why this timely book is a must read for Christian women who are hungry to grow and faithfully follow Christ. Far too many are missing not just the truth, but literally missing Him! Take Stacey's charge to heart; read, study, pray about, and share this book for "He is worthy of pursuing, so Chase Holiness!"

— NORM MILLAR -SENIOR PASTOR - REDEMPTION BIBLE CHAPEL, LONDON ONTARIO

"Paul talks about running the race with endurance, but that can often feel quite ambiguous. Stacey takes you on a journey through the Word of God, helping you ask the right questions; that you might not just "know" the importance of holiness, but understand how to practice, pursue, and even chase holiness intentionally. I can't wait to go through the study with some of the women in my life as we walk this path in His Spirit and to His glory together!"

— LAURA ZIMMERMAN - DIRECTOR OF PROJECTS AND EVENTS, GREAT COMMISSION COLLECTIVE

"I love this book! I value its conviction. I agree with its goal, and I wholeheartedly support its theology. In a day of *hamster wheel* chaotic lives in pursuit of the temporal, the call to chase after holiness is joyfully welcomed. Actually, desperately needed. Weeks writes with clarity, sincerity and honesty that is easy to digest and then powerfully apply. Read this book, but don't rush through this book. When you truly comprehend its message, your life will see God's path, know His power and experience His purity. It's that important."

— ROBBIE SYMONS, AUTHOR OF PASSION CRY, PASTOR OF HOPE BIBLE CHURCH, OAKVILLE ONTARIO

FICTION BY STACEY WEEKS

Novels that Glorify the Lord and Encourage the Heart

StaceyWeeks.com/books/

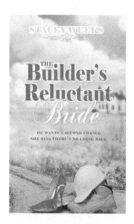

The Builder's Reluctant Bride

Fatal Homecoming

In Too Deep

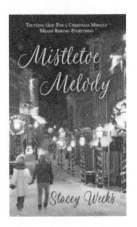

Mistletoe Melody

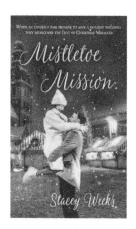

Mistletoe Mission

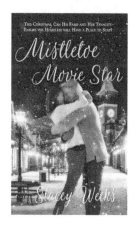

Mistletoe Movie Star

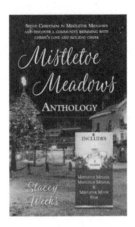

Mistletoe Meadows Anthology: Get all three Mistletoe books in one anthology.

Series Introduction: Sweet beginnings filled with endless possibilities. A short story sequence set in Sycamore Hill.